CW00859986

Emotional Intelligence

Boost your life by improving your EQ, Social Skills and Control of Negative Emotions!

By: Dale McLeo

Table of Contents

Introduction

Intelligence is something people often value when displaying their merits or their accomplishments. It is something that we look to, to display how much we know and how much we have accomplished. When we speak to other people, it is always the goal to not just show how intelligent you are, but to prove it.

The importance of intelligence begins at an early age, beginning with parental instructions. When you are young, you learn how to talk, read, and write. A parental figure usually is responsible for this, ensuring that you get the best chance to increase that ability to obtain intelligence. That person or persons will take it upon themselves to help you grow your intelligence and then show you how to apply it.

How we gain intelligence can vary from person to person. Many kids have vast intelligence before grade school. These people usually have had parents that repeatedly gave them encouragement, or instruction, early on. In these cases, children starting school can have enhanced intelligence before even taking a class.

However, intelligence is half the battle. It is only a small part of what shapes us for the years to come. When you are young, you gain intelligence from everything you learn. But you also learn to deal with rising emotions the older you get.

Recognizing Early Emotions

What are our early emotions? How do they affect how we handle life every day? This could range from anything, including how we react to a parent's affection or even punishment. Before we obtain the full use of our vocal chords, we express it with sounds emitted by crying. Once we obtain the ability to speak, we parallel our emotions with speech. We react to an authority figure with more emotion the older we get. That reaction can depend on what the authority figure is trying to convey. It is the way we emit that reaction that broadcasts emotions. How do we recognize early emotions? It can be something as simple as being happy for a small moment with a family member.

Our early emotions are formulated by how others treat us at an early age. It is the basis for how we learn to react to everything in life. How we recognize our early emotions can set us for life. It is also important to realize how we express those emotions at an early age. A parental figure will probably instruct us on how to convey those emotions, and how to react when someone tells you something. If a parent disciplines you, they use it to teach you how to deal with rejection and accept disappointment at an early age. This can guide us toward how we live our lives. It is important at an early age, because it shows us what we can be and how we can embrace our potential.

When we learn how emotions work, we reign them in. Much of this is because of our intelligence in accessing each situation.

Because of that, we gain a better perspective of our emotions and ourselves the older we get. Thus, we can gain a better understanding about who we are with each year of growth. But how do emotions connect to our intelligence, and what is it worth?

Emotions and Intelligence

We have briefly discussed the importance of intelligence and how emotions impact early life. But the two factors often come into conflict, especially when we are younger.

In this book, we will talk about how emotions and intelligence often come into conflict, and how they are difficult to balance. While it is difficult balancing out the two, it is possible.

We will discuss what we can do with positive emotions, negative emotions, and everything associated with both. These factors can determine how we lead our lives. The emotions we emit can impact our daily interactions with friends, family, and loved ones.

It all goes back to intelligence. The intelligence we seek can be good or it can be detrimental depending on how we balance that goal. We strive to be as good as possible at continuing our education and raising our intelligence. The intelligence parts of our brains usually create the area of logic that we seek to achieve. It helps us balance our personalities and create solid opinions.

We gather varying opinions throughout our childhood, usually with some influence from a parent or an older sibling. Often, it is just by observing how a parental figure acts and what they say. When parents are warned what to say in front of their children, it is because their children are actively listening to every word they say. Even when a parent does not believe that the child is listening, their children can hear everything that they say when discussing anything. This can be something as mundane as a grocery list, and it can be something as heated as political views and opinions.

It can have a huge impact on how we create our own views. What our parents say or do can dictate how we will act early on. When this happens, we act like parrots before establishing our own ideals. We continue mimicking everything our parent says or believes, whether our parents want it to occur or not. But that comes to a crashing halt as we approach the teenage years.

Once childhood ends, the teenage years happen and the rebellion stage begins. While we still admire our parents, there seems to be a growing discourse due to changing personalities and ideologues. That is when we express ourselves, sometimes loudly, and can come into conflict with the parental figures that originally influenced us. When this happens, we get into a bit of a lull. This occurs because we question everything our parental figures ever taught us. Our parental figures were our heroes, but no longer serve that role because of what we continue to learn. Our intelligence grows and our emotions spiral out of control.

Adolescence leads to adulthood. In the early states of adulthood, we are at the start of our peak, which also can cause arrogance. This is because we are still attempting to guide our emotions while reveling in our intelligence. We are at the stage in our lives when we are learning how to balance both. The early 20's in adulthood are littered with intelligent and emotional mistakes. We experience life and we make mistakes. Our emotions are still clouded, despite the intelligence we seek to strive for. These two once again will come into conflict with each other.

Our brains are not fully formed until we hit age 25. Because of this, what we could perceive as intelligence can really be us reacting emotionally to an event or an occurrence. When this happens, we get the two confused, and we do not really know how to respond to this. This confusion leads to us making all kinds of decisions without really processing what we are doing. That is why most people use their best logic as they form into a fully functioning adult. There is a huge difference between how a 19-year-old person would react to a situation and how a 29-year-old would react. The experience gained during these years teaches people how to react using logic and intelligence instead of emotions. However, some people do not learn to distinguish between the two. That is why it is important that we figure out the difference between them.

But what about when the two come into conflict? What happens when the two are interchangeable? When this happens, it creates emotional intelligence.

Chapter 1: What is Emotional Intelligence and How Does it Affect Your Life?

We have discussed emotional intelligence in many professional and social circles over the years. It has been a topic of many important panels and seminars. But what exactly is emotional intelligence?

Definition of Emotional Intelligence

We define emotional intelligence as the ability to control your emotions, and the emotions of others. While it would seem that simple, it is not. There are more factors that go into it. Emotional intelligence requires three important aspects.

The first aspect involves emotional awareness. This means you know of your emotions and know how to control them, without allowing them to control you. The next aspect involves knowing how to use this and apply it to everyday problems. Finally, it involves dealing with your emotions and also having the ability to handle others.

This establishes our emotional intelligence and with it comes all the attributes associated with it. Another word for emotional intelligence is EQ, which is short for Emotional Quotient.

An EQ is basically an extended look at someone's emotional intelligence through various assessments conducted across several platforms. Years ago, teachers gave this exam in person. In the current day and age, people use social media to help determine their EQ.

Experts use an EQ report to determine the most important factors attributed to a person's emotional intelligence. The five factors include: self-awareness, self regulation, incentive, social awareness, and social regulation.

Self-awareness

Self-awareness is the ability to recognize a situation while you are in that situation. It is comparable to you making a self-deprecating joke at your own expense. For example, you could also feel your emotions rising in any situation as you are experiencing them. Basically, you are in full knowledge of your surroundings and what is going on in your life at that very moment.

Self-regulation

Self-regulation is the ability to not just recognize what is going on around you, but the ability to control and stop it. For example, someone close to you could say something that could be deemed hurtful. It can be a very upsetting comment, one intended to hurt you. You would be able to self-regulate the feelings rising in you, thus not allowing the comment to harm you. You are controlling your emotions and not letting them cloud your judgment.

Incentive

Incentive is the motivation and ability to want to do something. With emotions, we can let them get the best of us. Emotions can destroy us from the inside and cause us to commit acts we did not want to commit. Because of this, emotions often are the biggest reason for people's misfortunes. For example, if you are in a healthy relationship, your emotions can often be the rise and fall of the union. If your partner does or says something that does not agree with you, it can cause you to react emotionally. That emotional reaction can cause you to say something you did not intend to say. When this happens, it can harm the relationship. Incentive requires the ability to take the next step to overcome this fallacy. It requires the ability to want to overcome your inadequacies and the emotions you are feeling.

Social Awareness

Social awareness is not just being aware of your feelings, but other people's feelings. While this seems like it could be easy, many people struggle with this. For example, you are hanging out with your friend and you greet them. They say hello to you, but you notice something is off with them. While they do not specifically state what is going on with them, you can tell that something is bothering them. It is your social awareness that enables you to recognize this and realize that your friend is not exactly in the best of spirits. Social awareness is also understanding how what you do and say can affect others. You need to know that everything you do and say can impact someone else's day. It is not just how you act with family and friends, either. Social media exposes us to more people than ever before. It has opened the floodgates for opportunities to speak to others, and the opportunity for our words to impact others. Let us say, for example, you are talking on an online forum with someone. You talk kindly to them at first, but then say something that can be deemed offensive. Because of this, you have the potential to harm someone's day, and maybe much worse. You cannot see how you are impacting someone, because it is online. Regardless, what you say can influence someone else.

Social Regulation

Social regulation is the ability to do something about how someone deals with their own emotional issues. It is one thing to recognize how your words can impact someone; it is another thing to do something about it. In your personal life, you do this by coming to an understanding about how your actions can impact others and resolve issues. It also involves building a bridge to communicate what we can do. In professional settings, this is important.

Often, we work with people who we do not particularly agree with. It can create tension and create conflict. This conflict can be detrimental to the work that we are trying to accomplish. Because of this, we have to manage relationships and accomplish the social regulation we strive for. We can get to this place by listening carefully to what others have to say and also understanding the impact we have on others. This can allow us to slowly influence others through our own actions. We can influence others through building relationships properly. For example, you cannot get someone to do what you want without resentment if you order them around. If you attempt to build a relationship that way, you will fail every time. Instead, you need to focus on how you can connect to the person you are attempting to build a relationship with. When you do this, you can break down barriers and form a real connection. In a professional setting, this form of communication can create a great working climate. Thus, proper self regulation requires being able to have a proper understanding of how you affect others and getting those people to come across the line.

What is IQ?

We have established what EQ is and the five important factors associated with it. Now we will discuss intelligence quotient, otherwise known as IQ. This is something you have probably heard about long before reading this book. You probably heard of what an IQ is on a television show or a movie. But what is an IQ? The standard definition for IQ is a person's ability to reason and how they come to that conclusion. It tests if a person can solve problems efficiently and effectively. What most people know is that an IQ is a score you receive after taking a test. It is a standardized test, similar to the exams you would take in school, only instead of one or two subjects, this test attempts to figure out your problem-solving abilities.

The American Mensa is one of the biggest distributors of IQ tests in the world. When you access the website, it gives you an option to take an admission test, review your past scores, or take a practice test. Once you start a test, they give you the fee for the test. Following that, you can take a test and see how high your IQ is.

The highest score you can get on an IQ test is a 160. However, that score is rare and not something you would see often.

According to American Mensa, approximately 3 percent of people who have taken IQ tests have scored higher than 130.

American Mensa also noted that most people who take the test round out to an average of 100. Their information revealed that about 70 percent of people who take the test score between 85 and 115. The rest of the people who take the test score less than 85. But how do these standardized tests work? Mostly, administrators compare the tests to other test scores, and then they curve the results. Because of this curve, most people round out to a 100 score when taking the test. But while IQ tests have become popular in media culture, it does not always accurately determine your exact intelligence. Often, a person taking an IQ test can score lower than they normally would due to several factors. Those factors can include the stress levels the person is experiencing.

IQ vs. EQ

So, now we know what EQ and IQ are. But what are the similarities and differences attributed to both? We have defined them and expressed the abilities applied by both. Now, we will use examples from the workplace.

It is important to illustrate how these two definitions of intelligence apply to the workforce. The workplace is where we go every day to make a living. It is where we are most likely to associate and communicate with other people. Also, it is where what we say and do can have an impact.

Those with good EQs are leaders, captains of industry. They are the people who will always have a great idea in a meeting and the ones who will lead the charge for change. These types of people are also successful, making the most of their opportunities and excelling beyond recognition. It is not just their success that defines them; it is their ability to work great with others and lead everyone by design. That exemplifies their great EQ.

People with high IQs excel at the most difficult tasks. They strive and achieve while others fail. These people are the ones that employers depend on to lift them out of bad situations, to carry their companies to greater heights, and achieve even more than ever before. Because of their high IQs, they can find a way out of any problem and master it beyond reason.

So now we know what the differences are between an EQ and IQ. This is where we expand our horizons and dig deeper into what emotional intelligence is.

The Elements of Emotional Intelligence

We have established what emotional intelligence is. Now we expand upon the five factors commonly associated with emotional intelligence. These factors are self-awareness, self-regulation, motivation, social skills, and empathy.

Self-awareness

Self-awareness is an important tool in the giant scope of emotional intelligence. You need to know how your feelings can affect you. They can take a mental toll on you if you do not acknowledge them. This is when they can become detrimental to you and your psyche. Self-awareness is the first and probably the most important step in all of emotional intelligence. You need to recognize your emotions and how they can cause a chain reaction. That chain reaction can be anything as innocent as a crying session, to something worse like a public screaming incident. Basically, you need to not be in denial and recognize your emotions. By acknowledging the levels of your emotions, you are establishing the first true level of emotional intelligence.

Self-regulation

Self-regulation, as stated before, can be tricky. Anyone can admit something, but correcting a situation is another level. A person dealing with rising emotions can be complicit in their own denial. The same person can admit their issues and still struggle to define what they plan to do about it. Admitting a problem is not the same as correcting it. You need to have a plan to actually do something about it. Is is comparable to someone who states that they will lose weight, but not actually do anything about it. Instead, they keep going down the same path that they were taking. It offers no resolution and no structure, not to mention no real path or plan. You need to gain the motivation to do something about it.

Motivation

Motivation is exactly what it sounds like. It is the ability and the wherewithal to actually go out and accomplish a goal from start to finish. You need to have the achievement drive to keep on the road and stay focused on what you are planning to do. That way, when you go out and start executing your plan, there is little chance you will ever go off course. Because of that, it puts you in a better set of mind. But to keep the drive going, you need the commitment to stay on the path. To commit, remain vigilant despite whatever obstacles life throws at you. Push everything out of the way and keep plowing forward. You must do whatever is necessary to accomplish goals. Also, you cannot let any obstacles stand in your way. With this, you have strived into your initiative. The initiative here should be to conquer your emotional hurdles and overcome them. Once you have overcome them, this gives you extra motivation for how you want to proceed forward with the events in your life. Because of this, your emotional intelligence peaks to the highest it will be. When you motivate yourself, you reach your highest potential.

Social Skills

Social skills are an important aspect of how you conduct your everyday life. They're applicable to your personal life or your professional life. We learn the value of social skills in grade school when we meet our first friend. That first friend gives us our first real test on how to act around other people. As the years go by, there are more examples of how we construct an even larger social structure. It is the basis for how we shape our lives and how we create our futures. By doing this, we go down a path of planning relationships and cultivating strongholds.

As we continue to get older, our social skills may improve and progress. However, some people cannot get to that level of progression. They struggle with their emotional conflicts which leaves them socially inept. This causes them to be socially awkward in almost every situation they are in, and this causes a chain reaction that blocks their ambitions. When this happens, it can create a permanently damaging effect and hinder a person from reaching their utmost potential. Thus, those who are socially inept cannot accomplish the goals that they originally strived for. It is important to enhance your social skills at an early age. Not only that, you need to keep growing every day and establish a platform for continuing to develop those social skills. For emotional intelligence, finding your social skills can be important. It can set the basis for how you react to others. Once you do that, you can establish a basis for empathy.

Empathy

We know empathy as a quality most people have. It is comparable to sympathy, where you feel bad for someone who has gone through something horrible. However, it differs a little. When you empathize with someone, you are forming a way to relate to how they are feeling. You are connecting your feelings to how they are feeling. That happens when you identify what someone else is feeling, especially when it is a negative feeling, and use it to connect to that person. We do often this when someone has lost a family member or friend tragically. It can also apply to other situations. You can empathize with a friend who has dealt with some misfortune in their lives, such as the loss of a job. It can even be something as mundane as a friend tripping on a sidewalk. You feel their pain because it is likely that you have been there before. The situation feels familiar to you because you have probably experienced it firsthand. Because of this, your empathy is higher and likely more sincere. Your emotional intelligence is embroiled by this feeling of empathy, and it gives you the ability to take someone else's feelings and connect with them. Once you have accomplished this, you can achieve the perfect level of emotional intelligence you seek.

Impact of Emotional Intelligence in Daily Life (with examples)

So, we have driven into the ground what emotional intelligence is. We have talked about what it means to be emotionally intelligent and how it corresponds to daily life. But what are some good examples of being emotionally intelligent? Let us start with the five core values of emotional intelligence. You now know them as self-awareness, self-regulation, motivation, social skills, and empathy. We will give two examples, just to set a different precedent for each.

The first example is one everyone has experienced at one point: heartbreak from a lost relationship. Let us say, for example, your significant other has broken up with you. They have concluded that they no longer want or need you in their life. It is devastating, and you are broken up. This is where emotional intelligence can come in handy.

To achieve self-awareness, you need to realize what your feelings are. You need to recognize your feelings and the effect that they are having on you. The breakup is causing you to act irrationally, not in the way you would normally. It could affect several things in your daily life. It could affect your job, or the way you are around your friends. A breakup often causes people to become depressed and despondent. Often, they do not want to be around anyone or even leave the house. Sometimes, they do not even get out of their pajamas. To avoid this, you need to become self-aware of the feelings you are experiencing and how they are impacting your life. You need to conclude that you are hurting, and your feelings are hurting you. They are hurting you, and they are hurting others. Because of the pain you feel from the breakup, you are becoming reserved and holed in. To achieve complete self-awareness, you need to know of your pain and not deny that you are feeling it. You must acknowledge it.

To achieve self-regulation, you need to be aware first of your pain. When you realize the pain you are feeling, you must control it. We are not telling you to bottle up all of your feelings until they one day explode. That would be impractical and unhealthy.

Instead, focus on slowly channeling the negative energy from your being and find some positives in your situation. It may not be easy, but it is something we all have to face in our lives. When someone we cared about moves on from us, we have to realize that the grass may be greener on the other side of the fence. It is not the end of the world when a relationship ends. It could be the beginning of something new. Maybe, once you look back on the relationship, you might start to realize that you were not as happy as you previously thought. Possibly, there were some holes in the relationship that no one acknowledged for a long time. Because of this, you see the reasons the relationship ended. It is not always your fault; it is not always their fault. Sometimes, two people just no longer are compatible. When this happens, we must self-regulate our feelings and take the next step.

Of course, the next step is motivation. Are you motivated to go out and move on? Can you find the energy and the passion to get going? You are now single after a devastating break up and you ask yourself what you will do now. Well, the first thing you can do is put yourself out there. Sitting at home and eating ice cream is not productive, though it may be delicious. Sulking and complaining to your friends does not solve a thing. You need to go out and do something that takes your mind off your lost lover. The first thing you should do is reconnect with old friends. You need to catch up with them and have the best time of your life. There are other social groups in your town that are always available to you. Groups like Meetup enable opportunities for people to go out and meet new people with no pressure at all. It is very casual, and a good way to help you forget about your troubles. The bottom line is that you need to motivate yourself to figure out how to control your feelings. Once you accomplish that, you can move to the next step.

Social skills come in handy here just like any situation. You have gone through self-awareness, self-regulation, and motivation. Now it is the time to go through the social skills you have learned over the years. How well can you apply this to the moving on process? You have come out of a new relationship. This does not necessarily mean you will enter a new one immediately. It just means you will go out into the world and apply those social skills you have learned. You should talk to a new friend and introduce yourself to people. Go to a Meetup and play some athletic games with different people. If it is summer, go to the beach and take in the wonderful sand and water. If you enjoy hiking, find a friend to take on a fun hike. Basically, this is where you put all your social skills to the test.

Empathy can be difficult for a situation like this. Let us say that you have gotten over your breakup. But now, your friend is the one that has experienced the heartbreak. They are the one crying on the couch, in need of a friend. This is where you come in. You need to be their shoulder to cry on, and the one to care for them when they vent to you. To accomplish full empathy in this situation, you need to connect your situation with your friend's and help them heal.

We have discussed personal heartbreak. Now let us speak about professional disappointment. You have applied and interviewed for that dream job. You are the best for this job and it is perfect for you. But then you find out you did not get the job. This devastates you, and it feels like the worst thing ever. This is where you start to question what is wrong with you. Did you cause all this? While this could be true, you cannot look at it like that. There may be other factors at work here that could have caused the issues you may go through.

Let us say the job you interviewed for had 10 qualified candidates. Those candidates all interviewed for the job and each of them made a great impression. Unfortunately, the employers did not choose you for the job. It was probably not something you did in particular; it was likely that the person they chose simply had something that they desired. It could have been anything. So what do you do? How do you handle the rejection from your dream job?

You take a moment to reflect on what you are feeling. It could be a mix of emotions you feel. There is a possibility that the rejection could depress you a little. It could make you feel unhappy and despondent. Your self-awareness comes in the form that you are acknowledging all the mix of feelings you are experiencing. You know of them and bring to light what they are and how they reflect on you.

Self-regulation comes when you take action. This is where you tell yourself that the dream job was not the right fit. It is basically you admitting to yourself that sometimes things happen, and it was not the right opportunity. This is where you tell yourself there will be other opportunities and chances for a job. You did not get this dream job, but that is okay. There will be another job that springs up that wins you over. You are giving yourself hope and not giving up. Like in life, one setback is not the end of it all. You will overcome this obstacle and rise again.

To do this, you need to garner the motivation. This seems like retread, but it applies in every sense. You must remain motivated to go out and apply for other jobs. You need to keep your spirits up and give yourself a chance to bounce back from this setback. This is where you pick yourself up and put yourself out there. So you did not get that amazing job, but you later find another one that you equally love. You do not have to put yourself in a box. Basically, this means you focus on your goal and you will find your ultimate happiness. That benefits your emotional intelligence and allows you to press forward.

Your social skills play a vital role here. They will prop you up to truly help you overcome your latest obstacle. When you can do this, you can easily maneuver from any situation to the next. This allows you to basically bounce from one situation to the next without being too destroyed by it. You are not ignoring your feelings, either. The situation still upsets you, but you are processing it in a healthy way that allows you to move on faster.

That way, you can accomplish anything you set your mind to, and achieve anything you desire.

Similar to heartbreak, let us say it was a friend that experienced the professional letdown. Instead of not getting the job, let us say that they lost the job entirely. They are out of a job after working there for approximately one year. You will try to empathize because you have probably been in their shoes before. We all have lost a job during our life. Often, it is not directly our fault to begin with. However, that does not change the fact that we are no longer in possession of employment.

Here, your friend lost their amazing job after one solid year. It crushes them, and they are heartbroken. Mainly, they feel this way because they loved that job and the people they worked with. However, they are no longer there because their employers slashed the department they worked in. So now they are venting and feeling down on themselves. This is where you come in. You must remind them they are an amazing worker by pointing out their talents and abilities. You must remind them of all the good that they have done for the company and showcase what more good they can do for another company. The empathy you show will reflect nicely on you, and it will enable your friend to appreciate you even more.

Chapter 2: A Brief History of Emotional Intelligence

We have discussed at length what emotional intelligence is. We have gone over IQ and EQ, and all the factors that come into play. But where did all of this originate from? Where did the term 'emotional intelligence' come from and who coined it?

Dr. John, Dr. Mayer, and Peter Salovey are the men responsible for coming up with emotional intelligence. They came up with this idea in 1990, when they were conducting research on emotions and how people responded to certain situations.

One of their experiments included having people watch a film that was disturbing. They studied how the film affected these people, and every emotion they exhibited. People who recognized their emotional feelings quickly were rated highly.

Emotional intelligence took off like lightning when their work was noticed by Daniel Goldman. Goldman was working for the largest newspaper in New York writing about scientific topics. He began working on a book about how emotional intelligence has a higher impact on the workforce than any other form of intelligence.

Now that we understand the origins, let us look at emotional intelligence on a grander scale.

EQ Model

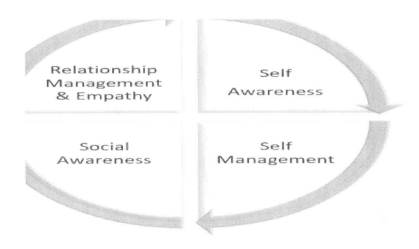

Why Developing Emotional Intelligence Skills is Important

We have looked at emotional intelligence and everything it represents. Now you know the origins of where the terms came from. You have seen the charts, and the figures. But one thing we have not discussed is why it is so important to develop emotional intelligence and the skills associated with it.

First, it is not healthy to let your emotions get the best of you. When this happens, it can affect you and others around you. It can affect you not just in social situations, but it also can impact your health.

Imagine you are playing a video game, and you are really into it. But you are so into it that you lose sight of the fact that it is just a game you are playing. You forget that it is not important. So when you scream at the television for something that goes wrong, you lose sight of the fact that it is just a game.

This happens often to people who watch sports. They watch their favorite sports team playing against a hated rival. During the game, they get so intense when watching the game that it causes an array of emotions. When their team scores, they cheer. However, when their team struggles, they get angry. This causes them to shout angry remarks, which can include obscenities. It also raises their emotional levels. While being happy can be a great thing, anger can harm you. When you get angry, it can cause your blood pressure to rise. It can also do damage to your heart and potentially threaten your life. Similar to video games, you need to realize that it is just a sports game. It is not the end of the world.

But let us expand upon that concept. Emotional intelligence gained a definition to establish how people react to their emotions. When Mayer and Salovey created this concept, they did it to understand human emotions and how they reflect upon the way we live our lives. The researchers wanted to understand why people react the way they do to certain things.

But why was recognizing emotional intelligence important? Let us go back to the origin of this term and why these researchers defined it to begin with. They did this to understand human emotions and how people react in a variety of situations.

Emotional intelligence is very important for establishing proper lines of communication. The best families have great emotional intelligence, because they have passed it down from one generation to another. Also, a solid foundation of emotional intelligence can create better harmony for all involved. It also means that there will be a better understanding of everyone's ideals, and their desires.

Emotional intelligence is important for social skills. You need this because you will interact with people in your everyday life. As stated in the intro, it all goes back to grade school. You start kindergarten; you meet your first friend. When you make your first friend, you establish a connection that you did not have before. The only people you knew before making this connection were your parents. Potentially, you had an older brother or sister. Maybe you also had aunts, uncles, and grandparents. But this is the first non-blood person you are befriending. This is a new experience, and something that starts your path to establishing several forms of emotions.

So you have made your first friend, and you make another friend. This friend will not be like your first friend. Likely, this friend will be a little different. That is a good thing. It is your first experience with something different. This is when you realize that there are different people in all walks of life. As you grow older, you form various relationships with all kinds of people.

You enter middle school and you make even more friends. This is where it gets a little complicated. You experience something you have never experienced in your life. This experience you feel is called puberty. Boys and girls go through it at different times. Depending on where you are in your growing phase, you become romantically interested in people. This causes a chain of emotions unheard of in your life before. When this happens, your teenage brain cannot process this all at once. You feel all your feelings all at once, with an attitude that you are fighting against the entire world. Because of this, you have not reached your peak of emotional intelligence. You are still in a phase where you are learning about your environment while dealing with other social factors. Once you graduate high school, it is on to another test.

You get to college, and you mature a little. But again, you are not there yet. As you graduate from college or trade school, you enter the workforce. That is when you see the levels of emotional intelligence you have. This is because you are now in an environment where you are being paid to do a job which also requires working with other people. Situations that occur at work can test your emotional intelligence levels and how well you process.

We establish social skills early to give us a foundation for how we live our lives. It is the way to create a healthy lifestyle and a better way of life. But what is the importance of emotional intelligence with social skills?

Remember that social skills are not just verbal, they are also non verbal. Anyone could say something to you and you could acknowledge it. That is easy. It is simple for someone to tell you they are sad, and for you to tell them it is okay and that you are there for them. However, it is a different story when someone is being evasive about their true feelings. You ask a person how they are, and they say they are fine. Normally, you would assume that maybe they are okay. But looking at context, and read body language. You must pay attention to how they respond. It is not just what they say, but the tone they use in responding to your question as well as their body language. A person could tell you how they really are feeling by displaying their dismay within their body language.

You need to establish your emotional intelligence not just for yourself, but for others. Your emotional intelligence is not just dependent on how you act, but how you act around others. We drive back the point that empathy is important. It is important for non-verbal communication and to continually improve relationships as you continue to grow.

But what about physical health? Emotional intelligence is not just about how your feelings are spiraling out of control. It also can impact your body and how well you treat it. Let us use some examples.

We are back to that breakup example from the previous chapter. Often, when a relationship ends, people cope with it by eating. The reverse also may be true. When people eat after a breakup, it usually is because they are trying to deal with the breakup. While it may seem like a television trope, people eat ice cream after having their heart broken. The cliché has actually been verified as accurate in many psychological articles. Ice cream is a dessert many people indulge in after hearing difficult news. This treat and habit can also be detrimental to their health. Eating fatty foods such as ice cream can cause you to gain weight. When you gain weight, it can slow you down, and cause you some issues you did not have before.

Those issues could include heart problems, stomach problems, and indigestion. When this happens, you gain a brand new problem. Because of this, it makes what you are feeling not matter as much because you have new problems to worry about. These problems take effect because you have neglected your body due to your feelings overtaking your logic. This is a good example of someone that does not have solid emotional intelligence. Their emotions control their actions.

Now let us look at people who stop eating completely when a relationship ends. According to a study conducted by E.A. Mayer ("Gut feelings: the emerging biology of gut-brain communication", 2011), the brain and the stomach are connected. When you experience strong feelings about something, it can overtake the logic in your brain. With this, it can cause you to do things you would not ordinarily do. For example, you are a person in good shape. You exercise every day and you eat three healthy meals a day, with no salty snacks. This is a common lifestyle among young people in particular.

Mayer's study concluded that an external environment created central responses. Those responses created gut responses, which then produced an intestinal environment. What this means is that something could happen to you that could shock you to the core. That could then cause you to eat excessively or eat even less. Often, when people lose loved ones to tragedy, they lose their appetite. How is this possible? The human body needs to eat and take in as much food as possible. Well, something in our emotions shuts down the part of our body that requires food. The overwhelming feelings we feel manipulate our bodies into believing we do not need food, and that is because we are feeling down. We feel down because our feelings toward our current situation are overwhelmingly negative.

It is important to establish strong emotional intelligence so your physical health stays intact. You do this by keeping up your routine. Do not allow circumstances to get you down and destroy you. You must overcome all of your issues and show that you are stronger. Once you accomplish this, your body will stay where you want it, and you will overcome the overwhelming negative emotions you are feeling.

Physical health is important, but mental health is equally important. We have discussed this subject to death, especially in America. But it does not negate the importance of the sensitive subject.

According to the National Institute of Mental Health (NIH), about one in five adults living in the U.S. suffered from some mental health issue in 2017. That amounted to 46.6 million people. The NIH showed that people between the ages of 18 and 25 accounted for approximately 26 percent of people in the U.S. that suffered from some form of mental illness. To compound that, there were 11.2 million people above the age of 18 that suffered from an extreme mental illness in the same year.

So what does that say about people in the United States? It represents a worrying statistic about people who are not experiencing a high level of emotional intelligence. The issues these people face overwhelm them and then affect them to the point where they suffer from a mental illness. So how can this be fixed? There are no simple answers to this.

But as stated in a previous chapter, it is important to not let situations in life bog you down. It is imperative that you fight through whatever huddle you are undertaking. You need to take hold of your life and overcome the issues. If you have suffered through something horrible, choose instead to rely on friends and family to help you through it. When you do this, it can help you overcome your feelings of anger, resentment, and sadness.

Once you overcome physical and mental health challenges, you can achieve better relationships. This is not just referring to romantic relationships. Establishing solid emotional intelligence can help lead to a better foundation with family and friends. When your emotional intelligence is solid, your relationships improve and you find a middle ground with whoever you are dealing with.

Establishing strong emotional intelligence helps you enable a better line of communication with your parents. They understand you as an adult, and you see things from their perspective. When this happens, you and your parents can both come to an understanding.

It is the same concept with friends. Let us say, for example, that you texted your friend. They have not texted back in a day or two. This could mean many things. Your first instinct is to either get angry or sad. You are angry because in your mind, you believe that your friend is ignoring you. To you, they chose to not respond to you. You get sad because you believe that your friend does not want to associate with you anymore. But remember, it is all in your head. You are overthinking things. Sometimes, you internalize things without thinking things through. Your emotions can cloud your logic. Remember, the logical part of your brain will tell you that your friend is busy. Life is hectic. We can all get busy and we will rarely respond right away to our friends' messages. It does not mean they do not care. It means that they cannot get back to you. Life can get away from us sometimes, but we need to always take a moment to breathe and realize that once again, it is not the end of the world.

Your relationships will only stay solid if you and whoever you are dealing with can establish a common ground. Misunderstandings are among the biggest causes of relationships being hurt. One person could get upset while the other would be none the wiser. It could cause discourse and instability.

Therefore, emotional intelligence is important to establishing and maintaining a solid foundation for relationships. When you do this, you can overcome any misunderstandings or complications that may arise in your relationships.

Does this lead to conflict resolution? Mostly, it gives you the advantage in getting to that point. You are using logic instead of your emotions, and it helps you and the person you deal with understand each other better. When this happens, it produces more harmony and a better way of life for everyone.

But how does this apply to the workplace? Let us face the facts: when you go to work, you cannot avoid everyone. Unless you are a scientist, you interact with people. If you are a police officer, you must report to your superiors. You also have to deal with partners for every case. If you work in a hospital, there are doctors, nurses, and administrators that you deal with every day. Likewise, if you work in a large company, you will speak with several people every day. This could include your cubicle partner, your bosses, or even customers. But what profession provides a situation where emotional intelligence is especially needed? People who teach for a living deal with the most people in their line of work.

Imagine being a teacher. Not only do you have to deal with coworkers and your bosses, but you have to deal with the kids you are teaching. If the kids are younger, it becomes imperative that your emotional intelligence is strong. This is because you are not just dealing with your emotions, you are dealing with kids who may be on an entirely different level. It fills them with various emotions and they act out differently according to whatever they are feeling on that day. That makes it difficult for teachers. They must navigate their own feelings while keeping kids' feelings in check. Not only that, they also must still teach those kids about the curriculum they are attempting to put out.

In this example, a teacher's high emotional intelligence puts them in a better position for success. It is not only their success that is on the line; it is the success of potentially 20 to 25 students they are instructing. Teachers have to resolve conflicts without struggling, and must be able to squash all potential troublesome issues that arise in the daily grind of teaching. Because of all they encounter, they have to hold their resolve. They must be able to contain their own emotions and be able to be a leader for their students. To be a leader, they must show the students how to act accordingly. During school hours, teachers are the responsible adults that students are around. They are the shining example that the students look up to, whether the students would admit it or not.

Teachers with high emotional intelligence can then pass it on to the students they teach. When a student has a good teacher, it benefits them later in life. They remember the lessons they learned from a fantastic teacher, and it stays with them.

Regardless of the profession, it is important to maintain emotional intelligence. You need to keep calm in any situation and help others prosper and grow. Once you do that, you can continue having great relationships with many peers.

Chapter 3: Emotional Intelligence in Relationships

We will dig a little deeper into the effect that emotional intelligence has on relationships, and that includes friendships, spouses, and coworkers. But before you interact with others, look at yourself first. Look in the mirror and assess what you are and who you are. Discover what you want in life, and who you want to be. Pay attention to how you feel and observe how to behave. It is easy to not notice the things we do and how they affect others.

We could say something that may seem harmless, but it could hurt others. Let us say, for example, that your friend asks how they look in an outfit. You casually tell them they look okay, not thinking about your words. Why would you? Something in the room has distracted you. It splinters your attention. You do not have the time or the patience to tell your friend, who you have known for years, how they look in an outfit. The fact is that you have other things on your mind and whatever your friend is fussing about is irrelevant.

We become comfortable once we have known someone long enough. It gets like this because we are at the point where we feel like we need not try. We need not try because we figure that our friends know us, and we know them. That is why something as innocent as a friend asking how they look seems ridiculous. It may seem ridiculous, but it also makes sense. It makes sense because the friend trusts us; they trust us so much that they want our opinion on how they look in a certain outfit. They want our validation to feel better about themselves. Now, what would the right answer be here?

You could be honest with them, without being mean. If the outfit is not great, tell them without hurting their feelings. Remember, we are all fragile human beings. Some people are more hardened than others. That means that we need to be told gently about something that we may enjoy that is not as great to others. If the outfit is not great, you need to suggest an alternative that may make them look better. Do not just tell them the outfit is terrible.

You need to manage the negative emotions that you may feel for whatever the situation is. This could apply to yourself, or others.

Let us use another example. Your friend is in a relationship with someone that you feel is wrong for them. How do you know this? You observed how your friend's significant other mistreats them. This irks you, because you care about your friend. So how do you communicate this to your friend? How do you reveal the truth about the significant other without alienating your friend? Perhaps all you have to do is tell your friend the truth. However, you must keep in mind that your friend might not believe you. They are in love. Their feelings are overwhelming them, and they cannot listen to logic. Despite the mistreatment, they love their significant other and want to be with them. So what do you do? Do you leave your friend alone and let them suffer? Do you allow them to keep being miserable for the sake of a failing relationship? That is not exactly the advice we are advocating.

Before you talk to your friend, look first at how the relationship affects them, and how it affects you. Also, make sure it is not just you that is feeling like the relationship is bad. Your friend's relationship may be something that is different, and it may be something you misinterpret.

However, if you realize that it is more than just you, and that it is hurting your friend, you must take action. It does not necessarily have to be physical abuse that is occurring. It can be emotional abuse, or a distant spouse. Basically, you are observing your friend's peace of mind. If your friend is miserable, then it may be time to take action. You can do this by talking to your friend in a way that will not allow them to rebel against you. Before you do this, proceed with the finest caution you could take.

When you talk to your friend, gently tell them your concerns. Explain to them what you have noticed, and that you are only looking for your friend's peace of mind. Reassure them you want them to be happy, and it kills you to see them miserable. By doing this, you are making it more about them and not about you. You do this because you do not want the friend to accuse you of being paranoid, or even jealous. They could do this because they might believe you want what they have, which is untrue. You just want to see them be happy with someone who treats them with respect. When you throw out your concerns, give examples of the behavior that concerns you. If your friend's partner has yelled at them, explain to them that relationships like this are not healthy. Relationships are about communication, not one-sided verbal abuse. If you have witnessed more abuse, then explain it to your friend.

When you tell them this, expect a hostile reaction. Your friend may not like what you are telling them. They may not want to believe you, because they are in such an emotional state of mind that they cannot see the truth. Often, they already know what you are telling them but do not want to hear it from anyone else. Their clouded emotions can cause them to reject anyone that is saying anything against what they are doing. Because of this, it may harm your friendship.

When they reject what you are saying, do not act hostile. If you act hostile, you will make things worse. Instead, try to listen to them and understand where they are coming from. Let them vent what they want to say and allow them to make their statement. Remember, you are attempting to help them. Arguing with them would do no good. Sometimes, just telling them how you feel helps, even if there is no immediate resolution to the conflict. It helps to just be upfront and kind with them, to show that you care about them as your friend. This is where you remind them you care about them. You have their best interests at heart, and let them know that you will not say anymore on the matter. Show them you just wanted to express how you felt and then let the situation go. Doing this will illustrate to them you care, and you are not pushy. It shows them you are putting them first.

Positive communication is always better than negative. This is because creating a tension-filled argument will do no one any good. It is counterproductive and will solve nothing. You must desire to help your friend succeed by the best actions possible. It is not something that happens overnight. Emotional intelligence is something that can be applied and improved upon over an entire lifetime.

The Importance of Empathy

We have talked about empathy. We have illustrated what it is, and how it affects people. But now is the time to talk about how important it is. As you know, empathy is the ability to understand and share feelings with someone. Unlike sympathy, you are not just feeling bad for someone; you are feeling exactly what the person is going through. You understand that person, and you can relate to what they are going through. It resonates with you because you have probably gone through a similar ordeal before.

Some people have more empathy than others. These people have all the traits of an empath. What is an empath? An empathy is someone that exhibits high traits of empathy.

There are usually several terms used to describe people and what they are like. An empath is the complete opposite of a sociopath, which is a person who does not care about anyone other than themselves. The middle ground between the two is apaths. Apaths are like the henchmen in movies about heroes and villains. They assist sociopaths with their games and do everything to make sociopaths seem like caring individuals. But empaths exhibit traits that show how much they feel for other human beings.

They are highly sensitive to the surrounding environment, and will pick up on negative energy. Empaths feel when others are in need. They can sense it and will rush to help.

That makes them intuitive. They understand their own feelings and know the limits to their emotional levels. Because of this, they can cope with whatever they are going through in a productive way. It enables them to take what they have learned and apply it to others.

Often, they are selfless. They care about others and want the best for them. Imagine that friend that always helps you. You asked them for a ride to the airport; they are there. You asked them for their help on a project you are working on; they are there. They came running when something terrible happened to you, because they care. Sometimes, they are more worried about your well-being than about what is going on with them. If something happened to you and you are in need, they will lose sleep for you. They care about you that much, and it shows in their behavior.

This also makes them very receivable to others. People gravitate to them. Others enjoy being around them and having deep conversations with them. Empaths exhibit the skills needed to make fast connections with people with little to no effort. Often, it does not occur to them to try to make people like them. This is because it comes naturally to them and they do not even have to think about it. They go out and talk to people, making a connection everywhere they go. It can often make others who are not empaths feel a mix of happiness and discomfort. Mainly, this happens because some people are not comfortable with this behavior at all times.

Empaths also can see through lies quickly. It is a gift and a curse for them. They can discover when someone is lying about something. They can tell when there is deception in the air, and often they will call that person out on it. Empaths have their own way of doing this, navigating the rough terrain and enabling a better connection. They know how to parse the waters that their friends cannot.

They also want to make the world a better place. It may seem like a fruitless effort, but empaths feel like they can change the world. They want to do things that can improve things around them. It is no longer just about their inner social circle; they want to extend their reach and help people they do not know. For example, let us say someone leaves their home. Imagine they live in New York City. They are successful; they are happy, and they have the love of friends and family. But they have the yearning to do more, to learn more. They want to go out into the world and change things. So they take a new assignment, in Africa. They go to Africa and help feed poor villages. They help people they did not know, and wouldn't even have the chance to know, had they not taken this assignment. The empath took this assignment because they wanted to help the many people who did not have the luxuries and the advantages they had living in New York City. It may be a small step, but this is their way of helping change the world.

Empaths also are always curious. It is not a bad curiosity. They want to keep gaining knowledge and enable themselves to be better people for the long haul. Empaths like to solve difficult puzzles. They want to keep solving these puzzles and passing these tests. It is a never-ending thirst for knowledge, and one that empaths like to keep pressing for.

One major thing that separates empaths from others is the ability to take responsibility for their actions. Sociopaths enjoy playing the victim. They love to act like the world is out to get them. Empaths will accept the consequences for their actions. They will acknowledge when they committed a wrong and make amends for it. Empaths do this because they are genuinely apologetic for their actions and will strive to excel the next time they have the opportunity. It also means that occasionally, they will take the blame for something that was not their fault.

Empaths usually are creative people. You will not see an empath working as a lawyer or someone in human resources. Instead, empaths usually will be writers or musicians. This occurs because they can work their emotions into a constructive manner. When this happens, they create great stories and songs. Imagine your favorite book writer for a moment. Think about why they started writing, and the stories they created. They were all inspired by something at some point, and they put these stories onto paper and created a book millions read. When they did this, you got to see inside their imagination and the ideas that formed from it. Because of this, you form an understanding of the writer. You gaze into the writer's mind and what they are like, based on the book they wrote. It is a lot more difficult to do this with lawyers. This is because there are two types of lawyers. One is a prosecuting attorney, or someone that is trying to convict someone of a crime. The other is a defense attorney, a lawyer that is attempting to defend someone from a crime that they are alleged to have committed. You cannot relate to either of these people because most people do not spend their days trying to attack someone, or defend someone. There is nothing spectacular enough in your day to warrant that atmosphere. But this is what lawyers do daily. It is their job, and a profession that empaths likely would not gravitate toward.

Empaths rarely like or get along with selfish people. They see the world as a place where people are capable of good. So when they encounter a bad person, it comes as a shock to the system. They are unprepared for this encounter and it leaves them uncomfortable and unhappy. This a new feeling to them, and they dislike it. By that virtue, they dislike selfish people. Imagine you are an empath. You have a best friend who is a sociopath. You did not realize this until you moved in with him. Now, you live together and you discover who that friend is. You know that they exhibit sociopathic behavior, and it shocks you. This is where you lose your belief in the good things in life. You believe most people by nature are vile people. While this is not the case, your relationship with this person clouds your views. Empaths and sociopaths can interact, but a long-standing friendship or relationship is not possible. This is because one person will care more, while the other will look to use the empath to their advantage. They will forgo the consequences and look to do whatever they can to take advantage of any situation. Often, the sociopath will use the empath as a buffer. Let us say that the sociopath is in a relationship with someone. They may use the empath in whatever lie they tell and that empath may go along with it, albeit unwittingly. This can cause all kinds of chaos. That is when the alliance between the empath and sociopath ends. They cannot sustain it for a long period. The friendship ends.

Because of their nature, empaths show more compassion than others. If they watched on the news that someone injured multiple people in a horrific accident, they may experience the emotions of someone who cares deeply for those people. They resonate with the people who were hurt because their compassion level is high, and they feel sadness toward the people. They know they cannot do anything about it, yet they still feel desolate because the incident affected human beings. That hurts them. Their compassion is genuine and something that they feel to the core of their bones.

Empaths also are cleaner by nature. They love to keep their homes and apartments as organized as possible. They cannot stand chaos, or a dirty place. When you go to an empath's house, you find that it is cleaner than most. If it is not, they will repeatedly apologize to you for the mess. That is because they are deeply ashamed of the mess they created, and the inability to clean it before company arrived. They genuinely wanted to clean but life got in the way, and they did not get the chance to.

They are often more tired than others. When you talk to an empath, you may notice their body language is fatigued. It does not reflect on their feelings toward you at all. It may mean that they have a lot on their minds, and it is exhausting them. This is because of all the energy they exhibit when connecting with people as easily as they do. Just because they can relate to people quickly, it does not change the fact that they are human beings.

Like a regular human being, they may need to experience some alone time. They need time to themselves to put their bodies and spirits back into order. This happens so they can keep their magnetic energy that allows them to easily connect with others.

Once they recharge their bodies and spirits, they are ready to go out and continue being a strong empath. Therefore, empaths tend to not like huge crowds. Have you ever hung out with an empath at a baseball game or a concert? They will have fun with you, but their energy levels will drain the longer the event goes on. You can tell when you look at them as time passes by that they are powering down. It's not that they dislike being there, it is more because there is only so much energy that they can actually give. They can try to hang, but their enjoyment goes down the longer the event carries on. Empaths can suffer from claustrophobia in that aspect. Imagine an empath that surfs. They look for the surfing spot that is not the best, but the one that is the least crowded. They do not want another surfer crashing into them while they are in the water because they would rather keep that positive energy they are seeking. Empaths do not want many people surrounding them and would likely try to avoid crowded situations if possible.

They dislike violence. This seems pretty obvious, especially because of their high amount of compassion. Empaths likely will not want to watch the news, or any content that has large amounts of violence. They are less likely to play a violent video game or watch a violent movie. Empaths choose the positive content, and the opportunity to lift their own spirits up. They are also less likely to be bullies toward others, or do anything else that can cause misfortune to someone.

Empaths love animals. They enjoy animals to the point where they treat them like their own children. This form of love is common with empaths. The willingness to care for animals is simple to them. Their goal is to ensure that the animal they are watching over is cared for and happy at the same time. Empaths dislike seeing animals in pain. Similar to their compassion for people, empaths struggle with seeing an animal in pain. They are not likely to watch nature videos due to this trait, because in nature, many animals hunt each other for food.

Empaths dislike when bad people get away with crimes. If they hear of a situation where a jury or a judge clears a bad guy of their crimes, they will get angry and fight for justice. Regardless of whether or not they are the victim, the empath will do their best to get the justice they seek.

This makes them endearing to underdogs, or people who are suffering from misfortune. Back to the Africa example, empaths want to help save the world. They want to make things better for people as much as they can, even when the odds seem insurmountable. They hope to see people who are struggling overcome their obstacles and succeed. Seeing other people succeed makes empaths genuinely happy. It makes their days better, and it makes them thankful for what they already have.

Empaths are free spirited. They are more likely to travel the world than others, seeking to explore places they have never gone to. The thrill of the unknown is attractive to empaths. You are likely to see empaths in places you would never even think of going. They gravitate to those types of places because they want to see what the big deal is and want to satiate their curiosity. This makes them seek places interesting to them and keep that curiosity buzzing.

You are likely to see empaths out in nature. They love the outdoors and enjoy learning everything about the outside world. They wish to be around the natural wonders of the world and seek to continue exploring beyond their wildest horizons. It helps them understand more about themselves.

Empaths also can let their kind nature get the best of them. Because of this, other people can manipulate them. This occurs when the other person does something or says something to make the empath feel guilty. For example, let us say you are the empath. You know this person who is a known manipulator, but they have children. You love these children and the manipulator knows this. So the person will get you to do a favor for them by reasoning that it is in the best interest of the children. You cannot help yourself. You love their children, even if you do not share the same affection for that person. But because it is for the children, you must set out and help this person. This is because you do not want to let down the children. Thus, this person has successfully manipulated you.

This means that empaths are too generous. They have a hard time saying no and rejecting a situation. It often means that they will be the person who picks up their drunk friends from a bar. They will bail someone out of jail if that person calls them. They will go to that party, despite not being comfortable around crowds, because their friend asked them to.

The best trait that empaths share is their ability to be the friend that everyone confides in. Who better than the most compassionate person you know to tell all your deepest, darkest secrets? They will lock up that secret in the vault of their minds, and they will not tell another soul. Empaths are the best people to discuss all your issues with because they can listen to what you say and give you sound advice.

Aside from these traits, empaths can manage all of their emotions. They know when they are feeling positive or negative and know how to channel it. Once they have recharged, they keep this ability. Empaths enjoy their alone time, because it gives them the chance to refocus their energy on themselves, at least for a small amount of time. When they do this, they can reconnect with what is important. This helps them recommit their focus on being a strong empath. Their emotional intelligence remains strong, and they continue to grow as human beings.

The Six Empaths

Many people have traits of an empath without being a complete empath. Often, people will share some empathy for certain situations, while also not feeling it for others. But how do you determine if you are truly an empath? There are tests online that you can take to determine how strong of an empath you are. These tests will ask you about 13 questions and then give you a score. Officially, there are six kinds of empaths.

Emotional Empath

First, there is the emotional empath. This is not a hard one to figure out. It is the most common form of empath. These people are good at noticing the emotions of others and picking up on what is going on with them and how they are feeling. Emotional empaths can pick up the same sadness that others are feeling and empathize with them.

Physical Empath

The next is the physical or medical empath. They know when someone's body is ailing. Instead of emotional healing, they move forward with healing others physically. Many doctors can technically be medical empaths. However, it all depends on what type of doctor they are. A veterinarian is likely an animal empath, as they enjoy healing animals. They seek to cure these animals of their illnesses and help them grow healthy and happy. Then there are medical empaths that help people deal with their imminent deaths. It is said that these people can bring comfort to the dying and help them deal with the fact that they will be dying.

Geomantic Empath

The geomantic empath is more in touch with the earth, and how nature forms around them. They enjoy being outdoors and love to explore new places. But it is not always just a nature connection. Often, geomantic empaths enjoy exploring places with a deep history and connection. These empaths will enjoy a place with a lot of history, whether that history is good or bad. They can relate to the feelings that the area they are in has experienced. Imagine going to the site of a tragedy that happened decades ago. A geomantic empath is likely to feel what the people of that time felt.

Plant Empath

A plant empath is exactly how it sounds. They love plants, trees, and a garden environment. But it is not just that. They also feel the plants and know how the plants are feeling. Because of this, they are good at gardening and usually have an amazing garden filled with the greenest landscaping you will see.

Animal Empath

An animal empath can connect to animals on a spiritual level. Think of any nature video you have ever seen. Do you remember seeing videos about the man that works with lions, hyenas, and cheetahs on a daily basis? People with these jobs are likely animal empaths. They have this unknown connection to animals that others do not have. They can gain the trust of dangerous animals, and care for them over a long period. It is not just dangerous animals, either. Animal empaths can connect with almost any animal.

Intuitive Empath

The intuitive empath, sometimes known as the claircognizant, can pick up on how others are feeling by being around them. They can pick up on positive or negative energy, without a single word. They can pick up on if someone is not telling the truth.

All these empaths can have a gift, yet their emotions can be overwhelming. They can control their emotions, keeping their emotional intelligence high. Because of this, they exhibit the best signs of high EQ.

Develop, Improve, and Boost Your EQ

Okay, so we have discussed empaths and empathy at length. We have gone over the different types of empaths, and how to determine if you exhibit some form of empathy. But what about EQ? We briefly talked about this back in chapter one, but did not go into specifics. So how do we boost our EQ?

The first thing you need to do is put a label on your emotions. We do not mean this literally. But you need to identify how you are feeling. Pick up on the emotions, whether positive or negative, and find a reason for how and why are you feeling the way you are. When you identify these emotions, understand the strength of these feelings. Take a moment to come up with an idea of what makes you feel like this. Once you have realized the reasoning behind your rising emotions, it will help you understand what these emotions are. Therefore, you will label them properly. You will become an expert on yourself when you gain the ability to do this.

You should take some time to identify your weaknesses. Find out which emotions are hindering you, and how they are affecting your performance. Take a moment to see how these emotions are impacting what you are doing in your daily life. You are at work, and you realize these emotions are rising. Because of this, the emotions can cause a shift in your work performance. This can cause a ripple effect in how you do your job. It can take an adverse effect on how you interact with coworkers, and even customers. When this happens, it may cause you to lose sight of what you need to do. It is important to identify your weaknesses and take action. You need to recognize the areas in which you are struggling in life, and work on strengthening them. How do you do this? You do this by taking a moment and collecting yourself.

In this aspect, you need to frequently check in on yourself. It is not always about fixing your emotions. We can fix nothing in a day. Sometimes, you need to take a moment and realize that things will not always get better in a day. You may have to go with the flow and realize that your emotions will be part of what you need to manage your day. They do not always have to be positive or negative. It is okay to feel sadness, or anger. However, what you do with this sadness or anger determines the person you are. Bottom line, emotions do not always need fixing. There will be times when you leave things unresolved. This could be the case if you are in the middle of an argument or disagreement with a friend. You will not always resolve issues immediately. That means you need to exhibit patience.

Be aware of everything. Train yourself to identify your emotions based on psychological reactions. Analyze yourself. It may seem silly, and even may be ridiculous. But we are our best analyzers of our own psyche. We determine what is best and worst for our own emotions. Often, we ignore the logical portions of our brains in favor of the emotions. Most of the time, we have to psychoanalyze ourselves when engaged in a situation that can be described as chaotic. These chaotic situations can cause a hindrance in our lives and affect how we live our lives. When this happens, it is very important to find a cause for this. Take a moment to analyze why these strong emotions are occurring. Why are you experiencing these emotions? Why are they so strong? And last, why are you letting them affect how you are feeling? This is where you have to have a therapy session with yourself. Talk to yourself about everything that has gone on in your life, and what you want to do about it. Think about the emotions swirling all around you, and how they can create a bigger problem than there really needs to be.

Identify an unhealthy recurring pattern. Take a moment to spot the issues at hand, focusing on one at a time. You need to come up with a logical conclusion to how you are feeling. That way, when you find the source of your problems, you can work toward creating a proper solution. What do you know about your emotions? Have you built the levels of empathy as previously outlined? You must figure out how to balance out your emotions, keeping them in check. Remember, you can always improve your emotional intelligence. It is not just how in tune you are with yourself. You must figure how you respond to others. It is easy to respond to favoritism and positive reinforcement. But how do you respond to criticism and feedback you may not necessarily agree with?

Calm yourself down first. Remember, not everyone will like what you have to say or do. Some people will always have a criticism to offer you. Whether it is constructive can be debatable. But let us say someone is critiquing your work. They offer constructive criticism on how to fix it. What do you do?

The first thing you do is take a moment to analyze the scope of what they are saying. Do not just focus on the tone of their words. If you do this, you will fail every time. It will be unproductive and you cannot understand what the person is trying to state to you. Regardless of motive, try to understand what the other person is saying. It may be difficult to do, because we all want to believe we are perfect. But no one is perfect. We all make mistakes and we are all subject to errors. It is an imperfect world and we are imperfect people. Be receptive to what others tell you. Pay attention and listen. Observe what they are saying and start comparing your ideas with their ideas. Maybe there is a compromise in the middle? Perhaps, your idea mixed with their ideas can create an amazing product? However, maybe their ideas are much better than your ideas altogether. Maybe what they have to say is so amazing it destroys whatever ideas you had. This could be hurtful, and it could be an insult to your ego. Therefore you need to shelve your ego. Remember, life is about the little things. If you only care about your own thoughts, you are less likely to have friends. Coworkers will probably not want to work with you at all. They would not want to work with you because you are not willing to hear their ideas. Think about that for a moment. Why would anyone want to deal with you if you only care about your own ideas? They will not, and that is why you have to learn how to deal with constructive criticism.

But how do you handle negative energy? How do you deal with the negative feelings you are experiencing when listening to a person criticize your work? First, throw those negative feelings away. We mean it! It is not worth it. Actively listen to what the other person is trying to say. It might be the worst way to criticize someone, but you must remember that it will not be productive to get angry. It would be a waste of time to even argue with the person. If you argue, it would probably aggravate the situation a little more. This would do nothing but make things worse, and you will have achieved nothing but another argument. So stop and cool down. Process your emotions and think logically. The logical part of your brain is there to help you make smart decisions. It enables you to process all the positives and negatives. The logical part of your brain keeps you safe and also helps you make more money. It also helps you decide which course of action is the best, and which is not.

Be assertive without being rude. Again, listen to what the other person has to say. Think about what to say, and the best way of saying it without being mean. Remember, you want to establish a two-way dialogue. It is a conversation between two people. It is not one person angrily yelling at another. That would be useless and probably sever the relationship and communication completely. Communicate your response to the ideas and establish what you like and dislike about what the other person has said. Ask questions. You need to understand why the other person feels this way, that way there are no misunderstandings.

Once you do this, you will take any criticism someone throws at you.

Active listening is important in any situation. We have used the work example, but what about personal relationships? Personal relationships can be tricky, but they can be very successful if communication is strong. For example, you are in a relationship with someone. You have overcome the honeymoon stage, which is the part of the relationship where it is nothing but love and bliss. This means that now you are in a committed relationship officially. Because of this, you now will have to overcome some hurdles that couples go through. It could stem from one little argument. Little arguments can turn into large arguments. This occurs if people do not communicate their concerns efficiently. When this happens, it leads to misunderstandings, and sometimes the dissolving of the relationship.

This is where active listening comes into play. You must take the action needed to be an effective listener. Establish yourself as someone willing to listen to your partner and what they have to say. It will not always be pretty. You could upset your partner with something as mundane as not picking up after yourself. Then, they call you out on it. Because of this, you might get defensive. You would then call them out on something, such as their tendency to take a long time to get ready to go out. This would cause your partner to retaliate and call you out on something else, and the cycle would continue. This is unproductive. It will strain your relationship and will not resolve your issues. Instead, it will create a shouting match, and no one wants that. So here is what you need to do instead. Take what your partner is saying and try to understand their point of view. Understand what they are trying to communicate and show some empathy. It is not the easiest thing in the world. Once again, shelve your ego and put that aside. Remember, relationships are also two-way streets. It is all about communication with your partner, and how efficiently you can communicate what you are attempting to say. This will help your relationship and increase your EQ while further establishing your emotional intelligence.

This is where you have to be accountable. You must reign in your emotions and focus on the productivity process. This means you have to logically assess what would make the situation beneficial for the both of you. Remember, sociopaths either do not have this ability, or are terrible at pretending to have it. Empaths can exhibit this trait, and mostly are successful at doing so. Understand how other people are feeling and access them through their emotions. Take note of what your partner is saying and how it impacts you and them. Learn how to cue in on what their feelings are, and how to be sensitive about those feelings. People are not all wired the same. You could be one way, and your partner could be different. How you react to what they say dictates what will happen next. Accountability is important, and it is the foundation from which we form healthy relationships. Get to a middle ground, where you can sway the conversation back to a friendly place.

To keep everything friendly, remember to establish the lines of communication. This can apply to everything. It is important to remember that you need to track your progress every day. Controlling our emotions is an everyday thing, with no imminent solution. Control your impulses to say something or do something that may get you in trouble. Figure out how what you say or do affects others. Understand your actions so you know to not repeat mistakes.

Body language is important. Showcase your body language and understand how others can interpret it. Imagine you are at a job interview. What are the rules for how you act during an interview? Well, body language is essential. Do not slouch or lay back. This gives a bad impression to the person interviewing you. They might misinterpret this as a disinterest in the position, or that you may be too casual. Because of this, you may lose out on a great job because of the way you sat during your conversation. Comparably, you need to identify how your body language reflects on you.

It is not just for interviews either. This is important when you are talking with a friend or family member. If someone is talking to you, and you are looking sideways, they will assume that you are not listening. Naturally, you reassure them you are and they should not worry. But in their mind, you do not care about what they have to say. This is because of your body language, and how you are presenting it to them. Also, your body language reflects in your speech. Are you talking too fast? Are you speaking too slow? Remember to track what you are saying and how you are saying it, because it could impact your relationships with people. When someone is speaking, wait until they finish. There is always the urge to cut in, even when you agree with their point. You want to get what you have to say out there because you feel it is important. Sometimes, we do this because we are excited about what we have to say. Other times, we do this because we are afraid of forgetting what we will say. It is not altogether wrong. It is human nature. We have a lot on our minds and we want everyone to hear it. But it all goes back to listening. Active listening requires not just hearing what the other person is saying, but understand it. Take verbal cues to determine when it is appropriate to speak. This can be difficult when speaking to someone on the phone. Mainly, it is difficult because you cannot see the person you are speaking with so you have to actively wait for them to finish, and may even have to wait a few seconds to make sure.

This is where practice comes into play. Actively practice listening to others and being assertive, not aggressive. What is the difference, you ask? Being assertive means you are confident in what you are saying, and your personality reflects it. It means you have a strong prescience in the room and in the conversation, and you do not have to try too hard. Aggressive means you are actively confrontational. You are not willing to listen to what the other person says, thus destroying any forms of proper communication. Instead, you are uncooperative and only want to hear your own ideas. This goes back to active listening, and how it is important to do so. You must practice being assertive, without attempting to dominate or control the conversation. Try to understand where the other person is coming from.

This goes back to empathy. Yes, we are back to that. It remains a vital part of having strong emotional intelligence, because it plays a key part in establishing great human communication. Practice empathy every day. Try to make a list of the ways you can empathize with another person, and how you can feel what they feel. Note the ideas and concepts others have and relate to them.

Improve upon your verbal and nonverbal communication. There are always opportunities to improve on everything in life. We need to verbalize what we want to say, and practice doing that every day. Often, we have to learn how to take non verbal cues. Then, we have to practice our own non verbal cues and learn how to improve upon them.

This is where we have to form a connection with the real world. Get off your computer or tablet and go to talk to a real person. You will find it is much more enjoyable being in the company of an actual person than someone you are talking to online. When you do this, you can actually see the person you are dealing with and potentially have a meaningful conversation. Understand how the real world works and what makes it tick. Set out to accomplish more goals than ever before and go out and do them efficiently. Make a checklist and practice your interactions daily. Set forth and do this successfully and watch how it improves your emotional intelligence for the long haul. It will have a great impact on your spirits and improve your social interactions.

Develop empathy and establish relationships with people in your community. Go talk to your neighbors. You might discover that you have something in common. What is the worst that can happen? If they choose to not respond to you, handle it with grace. It is all about establishing communication and putting yourself out there. Keep practicing this trait every day to get the highest form of emotional intelligence you can achieve. Establish yourself as someone that can empathize with anyone.

Chapter 4: Practical Ways To Use Emotional Intelligence

We have discussed all the factors and traits associated with emotional intelligence. Now, we will dive further into practicality and how it applies to emotional intelligence. So how do you use your emotional intelligence to boost your life in a practical way?

Self management and relationship management serve a great importance here. Stop, pause for a moment, and assess your situation. Examine where you are in your life, and what you plan to do next. If you are in a committed relationship, think about how your actions can affect your partner. Carefully consider what you do or say in order to accurately gauge where the relationship goes.

This also applies to the workplace. You are at work and have a project due by the end of the day. You are tirelessly working on that project, but more rush projects show up on the docket. This upsets you, only because it seems to not end and you have a lot on your shoulders. You grow weary and tired, wondering if your efforts are even being appreciated. You resent your employers. This is where you have to put your emotional intelligence to good use.

Pause for a moment and take a deep breath. Getting upset about your current situation will not help you in the least. In fact, it might make your performance worse. Remember, you want to make good decisions logically, especially in the workplace. In this setting, take a moment to look at the amount of projects you have on your docket. Take them down one at a time. We are all human beings, so we have to go at the pace we are used to. Because of this, we have to know our limits. It is not the end of the world if you personally cannot get to every project in time. Ask for help if you need it. We all need help and sometimes we resist the urge to ask for it. Doing this will also improve your relationships with people. When asked for help, many people would jump at the chance to assist someone. It is human nature to want to help your fellow humans. But one thing we have not gone over yet is how we use emotional intelligence to test our own health.

Ever visit the doctor? It is not fun. You are constantly worrying about what might be wrong with you, and you really do not want to know. It is terrifying and it can be costly. That is the number one reason people avoid the doctor's office. But your health is important. People with strong emotional intelligence realize this, but do not always act on it. As exemplified before, empaths care more about helping others and it can often come at the detriment of their own well-being. Because of this, establishing communication is important in matters of health. People often like to hide their health woes from close family and friends for fear of gaining too much sympathy. They do not want things to change and do not want to risk upsetting the status quo. This can be dangerous, especially if a close relative being there could be of some comfort to you.

Instead, resist the urge to act like this. Your emotional intelligence should tell you that others are capable of empathy, and you need not hide the horrors of your life to maintain order. Trust is important in any relationship and you need to establish trust not just in the good times, but the bad times as well. You do not just have to trust yourself, but others. People who do not trust others lead a cycle of behavior that is unhealthy. For example, imagine you suffered a tragedy at a young age. You are eight years old and your parents have both passed away. The only person left in your life is your uncle, who has agreed to take care of you. But there is still a huge void in your life. Your parents passed away and you have to find a way, at a young age, to move on. You can still establish healthy emotional intelligence despite the circumstances. A person could rise to the challenge and overcome any obstacles that life put in their way. An unhealthy pattern would be if you were to stop trusting the world after this tragedy occurred. Do not close yourself off from the world and allow yourself to lose faith in everyone and everything. Instead, learn to allow other people into your inner circle. Give people a chance to make an impression on you and form that trust that you lost a long time ago. We can build emotional intelligence over a lifespan, with never ending opportunities for growth.

Communicating and Dealing With Your Feelings

So how do we communicate and deal with our feelings? It is a never ending battle with the feelings we feel every day. We could wake up feeling amazing and wanting to conquer the world one day. The next day, we could feel miserable and not want to get out of bed. For most people, there is no consistency in our feelings and what will happen next. This is normal and part of what being a human being is all about. You must be ready to accept this and realize that not every day will be perfect. There will be days when you feel terrible and feel utter sadness. The sadness and desolation can feel like the worst feelings in the world. They can consume you if you let them and you must be careful to avoid going down that dark path. Try not to overthink everything and keep it simple.

One thing we have not talked about is feeling suppression. There is a delicate balance here. You do not want to overstep someone and be aggressive. You do not want to suppress how you are feeling all the time. If you do that, eventually, you will burst and probably go off on a rampage. Both situations are unhealthy and not productive. You need to find a balance. Find a balance that fits both angles and try to come to an understanding that will be beneficial to everyone. Your feelings are just as important as others. Just because you are sensitive to others, it does not mean you have to ignore your own desires. If you do this, you will never be happy. Happiness is always the goal, and to achieve that you need to maintain and keep improving upon your emotional intelligence. It needs to be a repetitive thing that never stops. There needs to be a constant effort on your part to keep picking yourself up and never letting up.

This is where you have to stop and think about the bigger picture. Think about how the emotions you feel are impacting your life and decide whether it is worth letting them do so.

Let me explain. You are driving in traffic. The people in front of you are driving terribly. They are driving like the worst drivers on earth. They are slow and indecisive. These drivers cut you off and are going 20 miles below the speed limit. You wonder how can people drive this badly and how can they get a license? You do not realize it, but your emotions are rising. Your anger is getting bigger and bigger and eventually it will consume you. Basically, you are letting people you don't even know ruin your day.

Stop and think about this for a moment. You are getting upset because you may be in a rush. Or you may not be in a rush and simply want to get to where you are going. These drivers are a hindrance to you and it is ruining your peace of mind. Consider whether this is worth it. Figure out why these drivers are upsetting you and process it from there. Take a moment to figure out if getting upset about this is really the best course of action. It does not solve your current problem. The drivers will still drive badly, and there is nothing you can do about it. Sure, you can always yell at the other drivers. There is that option. However, there may be consequences to doing that. The other drivers may think you are nuts and call the cops on you. Or, you may find a driver that is nuts and it can endanger your life. All of this is over traffic. You let your anger get the best of you and it could hurt you. Take a moment and consider if it is worth it. Is it worth it? Would you let people you don't even know upset you that easily? It is just a drive. Everyone has somewhere to go and people all drive at their own speed. It is best to go out and just take this in without letting it upset you.

You can do this by understanding your emotional triggers. What upsets you? Do you know what upsets you easily? It may not be easy to determine. We all get angry at different things. Anger is a normal human reaction. We are not advocating suppressing all your anger. If you do this, you will burst. We are merely advocating finding measures to limit your anger and control how it affects you and others. There are many forms of emotional triggers that we have. It is all different for everyone. For example, some people get emotionally triggered when someone breaks off a relationship with them. It can come as a shock to the system. Someone you adored no longer can stand the sight of you. They do not want to be around you as much as you want to be around them. It hurts, it really hurts. It is a feeling that you cannot control. You feel a mix of anger and sadness. This is because often it is unexpected and you did not see it coming. Because you did not expect this, it stings you a little deeper.

But what if you were never with them to begin with? It is hurtful to get rejected by someone you have an interest in. You have built this ideal and worked the courage to approach this person with interest, only for them to tell you they have no interest. They are not into you and have communicated that there is no chance for you. This applies to not getting that job you wanted, too. A human resources manager rejects you for a job you had hopes of getting. Because of this, it reflects upon your self-confidence. You take a hit, wondering where it all went wrong.

You can also get emotionally triggered because of helplessness. This can be because of a situation outside your power and control. Because it is outside your control, it frustrates you and this can cause you to get upset at the situation. You dislike not having control. It triggers you and you want to make a change. But you soon learn that you cannot. It is too late and you are powerless.

Being ignored can trigger you. It can frustrate you because you feel like nothing. Many people would rather accept rejection than have someone ignore them. Getting ignored implies that you are not even worthy of a response. This is the feeling that many job seekers feel when they apply for a job and do not hear a word. It is also the feeling that they feel when they actually interview and do not hear any feedback. This is like a situation where you are being ignored by your friends or a significant other. It is not the best thing in the world.

When someone disapproves of something you do, that can be equally frustrating. You can feel the disappointment resonate within your body. It can be something as simple as a parent asking you why you do something that you do. Or, it could be a friend criticizing something you do. We dislike disappointing people, and we dislike when others give us disapproving looks.

It is worse when someone blames you for something. Whether you did something or not, someone pointing a finger at you can cause your emotional triggers to explode. You feel anger and resentment and the first instinct is to defend yourself. Why would you not? You are being accused of something and you feel like the world is against you.

What about when someone is too busy for you? We have all heard that story. You want to hang out with your friend but they seem to always be busy. They seem to never spend any time with you. This makes you question your validity, and how much you mean to them. It can be an emotional trigger if you let it, and it can be harmful.

That can be equally frustrating if you are visiting someone and they do not appear to be happy to see you. We like to assume that when we spend time with someone, that they are enjoying our company as much as we enjoy theirs. That is not always the case, however. Remember, in life, not everyone will like you. Sometimes, people do not want to see you. It is not always your fault. Occasionally, that is just how it works. Some people will be happier to see you than others. This can also work in reverse. Some people will be too excited to see you.

Someone might have an interest in you and come onto you in a needy way. This is something you do not expect, and it takes you by surprise. You felt sadness for the person and the way they feel for you. In fact, this encounter may even creep you out a little and you can become uncomfortable. This feeling of discomfort can impact how you interact with the person from that point forward and change your outlook on them.

This also applies when you are in a relationship with someone. Whether it is a significant other, a friend, or relative, someone trying to control you can have a negative effect on you. This is because you dislike other people telling you what to do or how to act. It can trigger an automatic response of defensiveness. Your defense mechanisms go into overdrive and you seek the fastest way out of the situation. Sometimes, there are no simple solutions and you have to face the obstacles you are dealing with at the moment.

These emotional triggers have the same thing in common. They are all feelings that can either overtake you, or can be managed. It all depends on how you respond to every situation. Only when you change your response can you truly evolve and manage your emotional intelligence.

This is where you have to find healthy alternatives to the emotional triggers that ache you. Go around your obstacles and set a precedent for what you plan to do next. You need to find solutions to your problems in the most productive ways possible to ensure that you can successfully manage your emotions. The first step here is eliminating all the negativity in your life.

Controlling Negative Emotions

Negativity is an inevitable thing. We all experience negative emotions in our lives. It is a normal thing to experience negativity. Negativity can come in the form of anger, sadness, resentment, or frustration.

We could get angry at our current situation and vent to anyone willing to listen. Our sadness comes from not being able to accomplish what we want in the grand scope of things. We resent the world for allowing us to struggle. The frustration stems from the fact that we are struggling. Again, these emotions are normal.

However, it is not normal to let these emotions consume you. To lead a successful life, you must control the negativity going on in your life. It is not just about external situations; it is about internal thought processes. We are our own worst enemy, but we could also be our greatest champion. You need to learn to balance the negative energy that is surrounding you and use it to your advantage. How do you do this?

Start by overcoming all negative thoughts you have about yourself and your life. If you have failed at something today, convince yourself you will succeed tomorrow. Sports are the best analogy for this. A professional football team can have a bad season and be terrible. They can win only three games and lose 13 in a single season. Because of this, a lot of negativity can rise and the organization can get discouraged. However, the best course of action is for that team to realize that there are better days ahead. They can focus on their positives and try to improve on the negatives. That way, when they play next season, they can achieve more victories. Failure today is not the end of the world. We all fail at something. It is what helps us grow. We achieve more when we have struggled to do it before. You can learn a lot from losing. It teaches us the value of working hard, and gives you the ability to realize your limits. Failing can devastate, but overcoming failure can be uplifting and wonderful. There are many success stories in the world of people who overcame the odds. Those stories are proof that anyone can achieve anything if they put their minds to it. Not succeeding at something does not have to be the end of the story. It can be the start of how you overcome the negativity and achieve beyond your wildest dreams.

Overcoming negativity is important when navigating stress. Think about what stresses you the most. Could it be work and all the duties associated with it? Perhaps your family and friends are driving you up the wall? These things happen to the best of us and stress is common among everyone. You would be hard-pressed to find someone that did not experience any stress in their life. Stress could be destructive if you let it overcome you. Once again, take a deep breath and realize it will be alright. You will accomplish everything you need to do. It will all get done in due time. But getting stressed over it will not help you. It may even be detrimental to your health. The best course of action is to relax and realize everything will be okay. Take a moment and breathe. Anxiety is common, too. People experience anxiety for various reasons. Some of those reasons can include an important test or even going on a first date. It comes in different forms for everyone and there is no clear-cut answer to this issue. Just remember that you are not alone in the world and there is always someone to talk to.

But how do you overcome social anxiety and shyness? How do you accomplish this, especially if you are an introvert? An introvert is a shy, withdrawn person. These people shy away from social interaction, preferring the quiet areas. Before we proceed, there is nothing wrong with being an introvert. Many people with exceptional emotional intelligence are introverts. It is simply who they are. There is nothing that they can do about it. But how do they overcome their own issues? Shyness and introverts do not always go hand in hand. While an introvert can be shy, being shy does not necessarily mean you are an introvert. For example, you could be shy around people until you get to know them. Then they see you and the interactions become more fluid and you engage in more conversations with them with no issues. Because of this, this does not mean you are an introvert. Sure, you may be hesitant to approach at first, but you are still willing to explore new opportunities with the people you meet. There are ways to overcome shyness and anxiety.

Take a moment and process what you have to do. Do not rush yourself. Make sure your brain prepares you for everything that you will do. Do not get discouraged because of your shyness. It sets you apart from others and probably means that it takes a little more effort for you. This is not a bad thing. You simply need more time to adjust to others, and that is okay. Acknowledge this and celebrate how it makes you unique.

Do not let mobile technology rule your world. It is tempting in the digital age. Most people have smartphones, and it is almost impossible to resist the urge to stay glued on one. This is something relatively new over the last decade, as there was a sense of better communication in the past. But now with smartphones, you can look at the news, the weather, and even read comics on the go. Phones used to be for calling and texting, but they have evolved into much more. That is not completely a bad thing, but it can become addictive without you even noticing. There comes a point where you realize that the best way to communicate with someone is by stepping away from the phone. Take a moment and talk to the person next to you. Go to a coffee shop and meet new people. Go to the park and people watch, or feed the ducks. Experience some fun at the karaoke bar. Doing activities like this will negate the desire to be on mobile technology. There are alternatives to technology, and many of them offer a great avenue to happiness.

It is best to not let social media dictate any negative feelings or energy. When you sign into your social network, whatever it may be, you may see a friend of your posting pictures. These are nice pictures of happy events. You felt this weird twitch of resentment. It can fester and you are not aware of why it is even there. People post images all the time on social media to celebrate great events in their life. Sometimes, a friend has gotten engaged and wants to share it with the world. Friends also may reveal to the world, via social media, that they are having a child. They have received a great new job. This can seem like no big deal. Everyone gets through these portions of life, accomplishing whatever they can to succeed. But take into account the fact that this can hinder others. Not everyone is at the same stage in life. Some people are struggling more than others. Two decades ago, it was more difficult to know of how successful other people were. The social media age has made it difficult not to. People love to share their success with the world, and that is not a bad thing. Most people post about their success because they are genuinely proud of their achievements. But our emotions can get the best of us. We could tell our friends we are happy for them, while secretly being resentful of them, and wondering why we do not have the same amount of happiness. It is also normal to feel some form of jealousy. That is a regular human emotion. But you need to be productive when handling that emotion.

So how do we handle the combination of emotions we experience? How can we control everything that seems ready to burst? First, you need to ask yourself why we experience the emotions we feel. Why do we get emotional at certain events, while other occurrences spark no emotion in us at all? Some people could get emotional seeing their best friend get married. That same person might not get emotional at the sight of an adorable child. People experience their emotions differently and handle them differently. Every single person on this world is unique, in their emotions and the way they strive to handle it all. Because of this, it makes things a little more complicated. We are all wired to handle things differently, with each adept in different environments. It means that there is no one solution for every person. The best course of action is to determine what causes the emotions we feel. What situation makes you feel the most and what situation makes you feel nothing? This all goes back to emotional triggers, and how they reflect upon us. Everyone has their own triggers, and ways of being set off. When something triggers you, it is important to see the reasons behind this, and how your triggers reflect upon you.

This is where you test your emotional response against your logical response. You use it to determine the proper course of action. When making an important decision, it is best to take a moment and process everything you will do. That way, when you decide, you will not have any regrets. Decisions require logic, and proper thought. The best way to decide is to think about all the good and the bad options that will result from that decision. Once you do that, you will have navigated the situation successfully. It will show that your emotional intelligence is strong and you can overcome anything.

Chapter 5: Recognizing Emotions in Others

We have strung out most of the terminology associated with emotional intelligence. You are now a master of recognizing and identifying your own emotions. You know of the emotional triggers that you may face. This chapter will expand more upon empathy and how to recognize emotions in others. What is the best way to identify how others are feeling, and how do you help them?

It is not always simple. As stated in a previous chapter, people experience emotions on a different level at different rates. They also convey their emotions differently with no common traits.

Recognizing Emotions in a Person: Basic Emotions

So how do you recognize how people are feeling? First, identify exactly what they are feeling. Be able to determine the feelings they are experiencing to help them.

Robert Plutchik was a psychologist who authored over 250 articles on human emotions, and several books on the matter. According to his theory, the eight basic emotions are fear, anger, sadness, joy, disgust, surprise, trust, and anticipation. We will go over all eight emotions with several examples for each.

Fear

Fear is something that everyone has experienced in their lives. Fear is the feeling of being frightened and terrified of something. It is usually the result of being afraid of the consequences of what you are afraid of. It is a common human emotion that comes from the sensory part of your brain that warns you to be careful about something. You are afraid because you are cautious. It is not always a normal fear, but it still can make you think twice before acting on something. Extreme fear is called a phobia. The difference between a normal fear and a phobia is that phobias last longer. With fear, you can overcome your issue with no need for help. With phobias, you need medical help sometimes. It can be dangerous and even threaten someone's life.

Fear is the number one emotion you need to recognize in someone else. One of the most common fears is arachnophobia, the fear of spiders. Many people dislike spiders, as they are some of the most common insects in the world. You cannot help someone with their fear of spiders. However, there are several phobias that you could assist with.

Acrophobia is the fear of heights. Imagine you are hanging out with your best friend. You both are hanging out in Chicago and go to the Willis Tower. You believe this will be no big deal.

However, once you both arrive, you realize that the building is over one thousand feet tall. Your friend has a panic attack, because he has a fear of heights. You recognize these emotions and you strive to help calm them down. The best way to do this is to reassure them that everything will be alright and you are with them. People respond better to reassurance when a friend volunteers to take the plunge with them. That makes them feel safe and secured.

What about aerophobia? This is the fear of flying on an airplane. It is like acrophobia, but this time, you are not on a ledge but thousands of feet in the air inside an airplane. We attribute much of this fear to the fact that the person experiencing the fear has no control over their situation. If they were on a ledge, they could just step back and avoid the edge of the cliff. However, if they are on a plane, they have to put their trust into another human being's ability to direct and fly the plane safely. Often, they end up becoming sick when they are on the aircraft. Reassure them that planes are the safest form of travel. Tell them about the thousands of flights that safely depart and arrive daily. Inform them they are in good hands and the pilots are the best in the world. Regardless of the source of the fear, it is an emotion you have to identify in another person. It could be the difference between life and death.

Anger

Anger is a feeling we exhibit when someone or something upsets us. It occurs when our blood boils at the thought of what is occurring and we felt like we want to punch something. Anger is a normal emotion that could lead to terrible actions. These terrible actions could border on the unethical or illegal. This is because when we get angry, our emotions rise to unhealthy levels. We want to solve our anger, and usually with our fists. Likewise, is is important to recognize the warning signs of when someone you know is angry. Learn how to tell when someone is feeling anger about something. This anger could cloud their judgment and make them do irrational things. But what makes us angry? It could be a multitude of things and events that trigger this anger.

Your friend could be angry after they endured an argument with a significant other. It could leave them steaming and not listening to reason. You ask them if they are okay and they play it off like they are fine. The logical part of their brain has told them to tell you they are fine so you will not worry. But the emotional part of their brain is terrible at covering up the fact that something is bothering them. You see their face and you can recognize that something is off with them. Because of this, you need to figure out what to do. How do you calm down an angry friend?

The first course of action is to let them vent. Sometimes, venting to a friend is a healthy way of releasing the anger we feel. Likewise, when a friend vents about their anger to you, it may make them feel better. That is why you need to make yourself available as the ears to your friend. Make yourself the sounding board for them and give them the opportunity to get everything out there. Once you do that, they will go off on a tangent. It may be uncomfortable for you but it needs to be done. When your friend releases their anger in this manner, it helps them calm down a little. They calm down a little because they realize they have a friend who is willing to listen to them scream about the situation. It gives them relief that they are not alone in their anger and that there is someone there to share it with them. Because of this, you have helped recognize, understand, and remove the anger in a friend. Your emotional intelligence has given you this advantage, and it allowed you to help another person.

Sadness

Sadness is a feeling we exhibit during situations when we feel at the absolute lowest we will feel. We feel sadness for a multitude of reasons. People feel sadness based on how the day is going. Some feel sadness because of the loss of a friend or family member. It could even be something as simple and mundane as how events of the world are going at the current time. Remember, empaths can get sad about events they cannot control. How do you help a sad person? Let us give the best examples we can on this matter.

Your friend has lost their father. He died of cancer. It is horrific, and your friend has realized that they no longer have a dad. This is where you have to be very sensitive with how you deal with this issue. People share their sadness in different forms. Some people will do everything to conceal it for the good of others. Other people will share it, but not expect any kind of reassurance. How can you reassure someone whose parent just passed away?

The short answer is that you cannot. You cannot say anything to diminish what happened. Their parent still died, and that will not change. There are correct and incorrect ways to handle this delicate situation, though. Unless your parent has passed also, do not tell them you understand what they are going through. That is the absolute worst thing you can say to a person in this situation. It may turn their sadness to anger, and they may redirect their anger at you. There are no scenarios where you want that.

Instead, tell them that if there is anything that they need, that you will be there for them. Tell them you love them and care for them and will be there for whatever they need. This may not solve their sadness, but it can help diminish it a little. From that perspective, they will at least realize that they are not alone in that aspect. Learn to recognize when someone is exhibiting sadness. You must be able to determine the signs and realize when there is something you need to do. Once you do this, it will be easier to determine when another person is feeling sadness or any form of depression.

Joy

Joy is a wonderful feeling. It is basically a synonym for happiness. We experience joy when someone or something makes us happy. It could be a significant other who you love with all your heart. A parent or family member could give you joy by their appearance. It could be something as ordinary as a favorite sports team winning a championship. We experience joy in many manners and we express that joy through a multitude of ways. When we are joyous, we are the peak of our emotions.

Our joy is almost always a good thing, but it can also cloud our judgment. Let us go back to an example from a previous chapter. You realized that your friend's significant other is not the greatest in the world, but your friend feels nothing but joy. Learn to recognize the joy in another person, and if it is constructive. It is a human emotion that can amaze, but also cloud our logical judgment and make us do things we would not ordinarily do. People who experience joy while in a relationship often go above and beyond to keep that joy. It may make them do things they otherwise would not do, had they not been near that person. That is an example of how joy can change us, sometimes for the better and sometimes for the worse. It is not a bad emotion, but one that people should proceed with cautiously. Emotional intelligence is all about balancing the emotions, so we include joy in that aspect.

Disgust

Disgust is something we all experience almost daily. We could get disgusted at how ugly a building looks. The bathroom we use could be so horrible that it causes us to be nothing but disgusted at the look, and the smell. Our disgust comes from our brains, and sometimes by smells. We could smell something that has such a strong stench that we want to leave the room immediately. We want to leave the room immediately to get away from that stench because it disgusts us so much. In this aspect, disgust is a strong part of our emotions and one we do not expect to come into. Of the eight major emotions as defined by Plutchik, disgust is the emotion we least want to experience. It hurts our brains and hurts our nostrils. So how can you tell when a friend is experiencing disgust? Worse, how can you tell if you caused the disgust? Let us give another example. You and your friend are at dinner and you both seem to enjoy the meal. You ordered a burger and fries and your friend did the same. Then, you notice something change in your friend's facial reactions. They seem to hesitate to take another bite. You wonder what is wrong, and if you are responsible. This is where we have to analyze our own habits and check ourselves. If we are doing something that causes our friend to act disgusted, we have to identify it and correct it. With that, we must be able to realize when our friend experiences disgust and correct it.

Surprise

We experience surprise when something genuinely shocks us. It is sometimes a good shock and sometimes not so good. We act surprised when something happens that we did not see coming.

For example, your friend says they will take you out for your birthday. You agree, not expecting anything at all because no one goes all out for your birthday. But then your friend says they have to stop at your apartment to get something first. You suspect nothing, thinking it is no big deal. As soon as you enter the apartment, the lights come on and everyone yells surprise. This surprises you and you are overjoyed. Everyone planned this big event for you. It is amazing and overwhelming at the same time.

There are some examples of bad surprises. You could surf in the ocean without a care in the world. The only thing you expect to catch is a nice wave. While you are surfing, you accidentally step on a stingray. This causes you to get hurt and feel great pain. This is a terrible surprise, and one you did not expect nor want.

Another form of surprise can come when we read or watch fiction entertainment. You could invest yourself in the storyline and genuinely not believe it when something occurs that you didn't see coming. It comes as a shock and you are unprepared for it.

The shocking event can leave you thinking about it long afterward, and it can impress you with how surprised you were. You can tell when someone experiences surprise. All you have to do is examine their face. A person's face can be the biggest indicator of how they are feeling. Sometimes, their jaw will hang open as a reaction to the event. They cannot contain themselves, as this is a natural reaction for them. This is the essence of surprise. In life, we experience surprises all the time. It is how we react to them that determines the people we are, and the people we want to become.

Trust

Trust is probably the most important emotion in the world. It represents faith and the ability to rely on another person. So how do you recognize someone's ability to trust you? How can you tell if you have gained the full unconditional faith that someone has placed in you? Well, you can gauge this by several measures. Let us use examples once more.

You have a friend that has a child or pet. They ask you to watch over them while they are on vacation or at an event. This illustrates to you that your friend can rely on you. They think you can care for someone they care for. That is a good sign and a great indicator of trust. It shows that you are worthy of being in your friend's circle, and they value you. Gaining someone's trust is not always easy. Sometimes, you must work for it and earn it in various ways. You can make inroads with a person by establishing that you are reliable. What this means is that you will execute something to perfection when asked. This can apply to personal life and the professional life. When you gain someone's trust, you become someone who they see as their confidant. They will ask you to do things they would not ask others, and it usually is an honor.

You need to earn trust. People cannot give it to you right away. You can determine whether someone trusts you based on their actions. Their body language around you is a huge indicator of where they are in their trust, and how much faith they have in you. Our emotional intelligence rises with how we react to trust, and how much trust we show in each other.

Anticipation

Anticipation comes when we are expecting something, and we are actively excited about. It is something that has not happened yet, but we are gearing for it to happen and we are excited about it. Imagine you are going to Brazil for a trip. You love the idea because you have never been to Brazil and are ready to explore a brand new horizon. It is an adventure you are gearing up for and one that leaves you excitedly expecting everything. You cannot contain your anticipation because the trip is still a week and a half away and you just want it to be here. Anticipation is a good thing, but can be negative if you allow it to overcome everything you are doing. It can also leave you with a sour taste in your mouth when your anticipations do not match the reality of what is occurring, and it disappoints you. Learn how to understand when someone is expecting something. You should identity when someone experiences this emotion and they cannot focus on anything but the upcoming event. It is normal to be excited, but also remember that you cannot allow your excitement and anticipation to overcome what is going on. Part of being human means understanding how all your emotions work and how they prepare you for every situation. The eight major emotions as displayed in this text all act as different behavior we exhibit when feeling some sensation. It is important to learn how others experience these emotions and also how to deal with people while navigating your own. You must navigate how you feel about someone in a particular situation and how it could affect you and the relationship you seek to have.

Additional Emotions

Jealousy

We briefly touched upon jealousy. We typically see it as a negative emotion and one that is frowned upon. The reason for this is that it stems from hurt feelings and resentment from one person toward another's perceived success. When you notice that a friend just got a great job and has a great relationship, it is normal to be a little jealous. It would be difficult to not experience a little jealousy when realizing someone else's success. It is especially easy for this to occur when you are not having the most successful time in your life. This is normal, and it does not make you a terrible person. However, there must be a line in the sand. You must learn how to balance your happiness for your friend and your jealousy. Find positive ways to show your friend you are excited for them. Do not isolate yourself from your friend because of their success. They shared their success with you because they are proud of themselves and want your reassurance. It may seem strange, but that is essentially what they are seeking. Most people are not terrible and do not share their success to rub it in. They want to gauge how other people feel about it. They want your approval and your commendations. This is the part where you have to acknowledge your friend's achievement and wish them even more success for the future. That way, when it is your turn, they likely will return the favor. We balance happiness and jealousy often, especially with our friends and family. What about shame?

Shame

Often, we feel shame when we've done something that we feel would disappoint someone. This happens a lot during childhood and adolescent years. It is common because we are still in the stages of growing up. We are still making many mistakes without thinking about the consequences. It is only after the incident happens that we realize the consequences and how they affect our situation. This can cause shame and make us regret what happened. This is because we have a conscience and we inherently want to do good, mostly. We want to succeed and we want to make people proud of us. So when we fail, we become disappointed in ourselves. It harms us emotionally and mentally, because we are capable of much more. This escalates when someone actually tells us we disappoint them. Remember growing up and hearing a parent tell you those exact words? We would do something that was bad, and our parents would shame us into feeling bad about it. Mostly, it worked to perfection. We felt terrible about what we did and strived to fix whatever the issue was. Then, we could achieve that level of forgiveness that we sought.

Embarrassment

Embarrassment is something we all have felt in our lives. It means that we have done something that made us look silly. This usually is done by accident and not something we intended. The logical part of our brain usually prevents us from doing something that could be perceived as embarrassing. It does all it can to stop us from doing things we might regret. So how can you tell if someone experiences this? Well, again, look at their faces. When someone "turns red" they usually feel some humiliation. Anxiety causes this at the current situation, usually brought on by embarrassment. When you are in high school, it could have occurred when you looked dumb in front of your crush. Or, it could have occurred when the teacher called you to answer a question and you were not paying attention. Thus, this makes you look dumb, and you get embarrassed at getting caught in this predicament. The embarrassment levels are not just relegated to high school, either. We can feel embarrassed if something happens to us we did not expect. Say it's raining, you are walking down the street and fall into a puddle, and there are many people there watching you. Or, you are playing basketball with your friends and you miss every single shot you take. When a friend experiences embarrassment, it is best to reassure them that everything will be okay. Remind them that it is normal and that you will look back on this event and laugh about it. This may simmer their emotions down and you will feel stronger.

Contempt

Contempt is a feeling that is worse than anger, fear, and resentment combined. This means you do not even feel that the object is worthy of deserving an emotion. It means that the object to you is worthless and not worth discussing. People feel contempt for objects they perceive as worse than them. It is not the healthiest emotion in the world, as it broadens distrust and resentment. It can be stressful and unproductive.

Let us say, for example, that a person is walking down the street. They see a homeless person. The homeless person probably asks for money or food. The person instead sneers at the homeless person, showing their contempt for them. It is an emotion filled with apathy and hatred. People show contempt at situations they are not interested in. For example, someone could show contempt for an entire country basing it on the reasoning that it is so bad that it is not worth visiting. Other times, people can show contempt for the job they are at. Many people are unhappy at their workplace. Some of them show it daily by doing their jobs without caring about the results and the consequences of how they do their job. Their contempt is so strong they have lost all interest in appeasing themselves or others. This causes them to do their job badly because they lack the interest or the motivation to do it right. If you notice your friend acting this way, there are ways to help them without offending them. Offer to help them get a job that makes them happy. Reach out to them and show them what they could do to achieve something other than what they are feeling now. This way, they can find a productive way to manage their contempt and focus on something that interests them instead.

Relief

Relief is the feeling of being relaxed after overcoming a situation fraught with anxiety. It is the feeling of being away from the stress that you were worried about and overcoming the obstacle that worried you. People feel relief when they pass a driving test. They often feel relieved after they pass an endurance test that leaves them breathless. It can also occur when they avoid a catastrophe that could have hurt them in a terrible manner. This sensation is their body and emotions realizing how close they came to losing, and how glad they are that they did not. You can tell someone feels relief by how they react to something and what they say. It is an indicator that they are happy to be out of a sticky situation.

Satisfaction

Satisfaction is the feeling of being accomplished and feeling proud of yourself for something. We express it when we are proud of what we did or something someone else did. When people feel satisfaction, they declare that they approved of everything that occurred previously. You can tell when someone feels satisfaction based on how they react to a certain situation. Your friend could have entered the house from building something and asked to show you the project. When they showed you the project, they could display their satisfaction based on how they beam with pride about the project and how much they adore their own efforts. This works with friends, too. You could feel satisfaction at how a friend helped you and commend them for their efforts. This leads to them being satisfied with your being grateful. It is a never-ending cycle.

This all goes back to verbal communication. We form the best relationships when we can communicate with each other, as well as when we form trust and respect. With trust and respect, there are no limits to how many relationships grow. When relationships grow, we are happier individuals.

Social Skills

That leads us back to socialization and social skills. We practice these skills every day. We could be at the coffee shop ordering an iced coffee with that white chocolate sauce we adore. Our skills grow when we thank the person who made the coffee and salute them for their great work. We do this because of our common nature and our willingness to grow as human beings. Once more, this all goes back to listening. The coffee-shop example is perfect because it illustrates how you need to verbally communicate what you want and also be able to listen carefully while the barista repeats the order. The barista will tell you the price and you need to pay the amount owed. When you do this, you will show how you understand the basic forms of communication. You heard what the price was and therefore took money out of your pocket and paid for your transaction. The barista's body language may differ from day-to-day but they will always try to assist you to the best of their abilities.

People experience different stress levels based on various situations. Our working lives could be stressful. It could be an environment where we are always on the phone talking to people. That could be simple for some people and stressful for others. It is best to see what stresses you out and practice the ways to balance that. You cannot allow your stress to affect others. Likewise, you must be able to tell when a friend is experiencing stress. When someone you know is stressed out, do not annoy them. That may seem comical but some people cannot understand when a friend is experiencing high levels of stress. They are oblivious to their friend's issues and ignore the friend's high stress levels. Therefore, you need to inspect your friend when talking to them. Analyze them for a moment and pick up on stress levels. If their stress levels are high, try a calming activity that might bring their energy levels down a little. Remember, you want to help your friend, not upset them further. This is best accomplished when you can discover how to relate to your friend. Maybe tell your friend a story that can make them laugh. It is said that laughter is the best medicine for anything. This could prove useful in calming down a friend who is not having a good day.

You need to create an environment that is positive and drama-free. It is not just about recognizing your friend's emotions and how they feel, but actively helping them. This is where you use your own emotional intelligence and put it to good use. You can illustrate this by being filled with positive energy and sharing good stories with your friend. People respond well to positivity and it will show in how you interact with your friend.

We discussed anger before and the unforeseen consequences it can have on something. This is because when we get angry, our emotions spiral off in all directions. A little anger is not a bad thing, but you must know when to get mad and when to not get mad.

For example, if your boss says something that angers you, you need to calm down before you respond. If you say something that others could misinterpret as threatening or insulting, it could cost you your job. When you lose your job, you lose your source of income. When you lose your source of income, you lose the ability to pay for anything you need. It is a trickle-down effect. Consider your emotions. Analyze what could go wrong and plan accordingly. There are ways to get mad in a civilized way without biting someone's head off. Anger is not productive when attempting to reach a goal and will not help you. Instead, practice coming to an agreement. Think about how you want to reach a certain plateau and approach it with a compromise. For example, your boss wants you to finish all of your work without overtime. They say that under absolutely no circumstances can you stay after work to finish this project. According to them, it can be done in the timeframe. But your boss did not take into account the fact that your other supervisors have given you added work. Your responsibilities have increased in your time there and it is affecting your work on a grand scale. So what do you tell them? A good compromise would be for you to inform your boss that you could do the work better if you had a partner or an assistant. Convince your boss that if they do not want to hire someone, they could always promote someone to help you. You know enough to train someone on the basics and it would help you immensely. This would work because you are saving your boss money and you also are actively taking responsibility. You are not making excuses, but offering alternatives. This also treats your anger because you used it productively and prevent a situation from escalating.

This attitude may even prevent future disagreements. It illustrates that you are a person of action and are willing to decide. You will take the chance on something else, and you will work around the boss's rules. When you do this, you stand out.

Conclusion

Emotional intelligence is all about balancing your emotions and establishing a healthy way of living. It is the foundation for conquering all your emotions and balancing them to the best of your abilities. The balance comes from how you react to every situation and calm your nerves when faced with a hurdle. That hurdle can overwhelm, but how you tackle it dictates the person you are. It displays the person you want to become and the people you would like to influence. While no one is perfect, achieving emotional intelligence can help your life and improve everything in it. It is all about setting a goal and executing that and then plowing further with what you hope to achieve.

Achieving Complete Emotional Intelligence

You did it! You have now achieved complete emotional intelligence. This is a testament to how much you've learned and the knowledge you sought. Achieving complete emotional intelligence is not an easy thing to do, and it takes a lot of patience. You must work on yourself every day and be ready to admit you have emotions to work on. Managing emotions is something we do all the time, and something we have to balance. We balance our emotions when we encounter various people at different times. This occurs because it is the safest way to maintain relationships. We do this by compromising our own emotions and our actions based on how other people feel.

We can go off how other people feel because we have empathy. Our empathy puts us in an ideal position to analyze and gauge how others react to us. By doing this, we are establishing a new precedent for accomplishing strong emotional intelligence. This helps us relate better to others. Someone could be sad because they lost a family member. Our empathy allows us to console the person without being condescending or thoughtless. We show our ability to relate to someone through their loss and come up with the ability to help them. Helping people is a strong sign of empathy. It shows that you actively want to ensure that the person you know gets your help. You give them your help because you care for them and want what is best for them. Because you want what is best for them, you do anything in your power to help them get there.

People love sharing stories. Sharing stories bonds us together and helps us overcome tough times. Think of any tragedy in history. People associated with a tragedy come together after sharing stories from the incident. It is not always a pretty picture of life, but something wonderful can come out of something horrible. When this happens, it is a proud display of how human nature can come together in the worst of times. It shows that we as a human race can unite when the odds are against us. Sometimes, we take a break from all the infighting to realize that we are all human beings going after the same goal. We just want stability and happiness. That is usually stemming from emotional intelligence. The broad goal is to always achieve emotional intelligence and find a balance in our lives.

You've achieved complete emotional intelligence when you have learned how to balance your own emotions and how you handle others. It is a sign of maturity and growth when you can do this. People will gravitate toward you and they will see you as the person everyone bonds with. This goes back to our section on empaths, and all the emotional connotations associated with it.

Emotional intelligence is not simplistic, as there are many variations to the concept. When you have achieved emotional intelligence, you notice a difference in your relationships. The difference shows based on the way you interact with people and how they interact with you. The interactions in your life become more profound and then you felt better about yourself. People are all wired differently in how they communicate with each other. They are like this because each person has had a different upbringing, and has a different personality. It is a mix of nature versus nurture.

As stated in the early chapters, our parents influence us early on. We take on traits similar to the people who raised us. Because of this, we do not show our own individual traits until grade school. As we grow, we continue to develop our personalities and establish our emotional intelligence. This enables us to continue to develop every day and become better people by that result.

When we do this, we continue to form new relationships with people we meet. Every new person we meet is an opportunity to develop a new relationship, and a chance to keep establishing our EQ levels. This helps our emotional intelligence on a grand scale and enables us to keep improving ourselves. When we improve ourselves, we learn new things. When we learn these new things, we have time to apply everything we have learned. Emotional intelligence is a good testament to how much you can learn and how much you can take in. It is also is a good indicator of how emotionally stable you are. But being emotionally stable is not the only thing you need to be. Once you have established your emotional intelligence, you need to learn how to apply it.

Applying What You Learned

So you have great emotional intelligence. Now what do you do? You take everything you have learned about yourself and others and apply it. Learn to take everything you know and make the most of it. Everywhere you go, make the most of what you know and how to use it. When you spend time with your family, analyze everything you have picked up and make use of it. Listen to your sister vent to you about her children and her husband. When your mother speaks to you about something important to her, take in what she says and relate to her. Your nephew is a child, yet even something he says can have an impact. Apply your emotional intelligence to relate to what the child is saying and use it to help him.

You are now displaying what you have gained from the world and redistributing it back. It is always important to share any knowledge you have ever learned and show others the way. Be empathetic to how others feel, as there are still people out there attempting to learn the way. Not everyone will reach the same levels of emotional intelligence at the same time as you do. You must always be prepared to handle a different situation all the time. People are all unique. This means that you will never run into the same two people in any day. That would be boring and take the fun out of life. Because of this, it makes achieving emotional intelligence challenging. It also makes it more enticing. This becomes enticing because challenges can provide new avenues for success stories.

Think about your workplace situation. Your emotional intelligence could be the reason your business has skyrocketed in sales. It could be because of your ability to convey a message out to consumers. Because of this, it gains you more respect and admiration than you ever thought possible. Situations like this can only put you in a good light and give you more opportunities to keep practicing everything all the time. Apply all you know and give back.

Emotional intelligence is achievable and not something that ever ends. Just because you have achieved emotional intelligence, it does not mean you stop learning. Always strive to pick up something new every day and increase your ability to relate to your fellow human beings.

When you have reached the peak of emotional intelligence, you become a better person and a better friend to all who know you. It also means that you are ready to show the world what you know, and are ready to help the world apply all you know. Once you do this, you can establish emotional intelligence for multiple people.

References

Diffen (n.d.) EQ vs. IQ. Retrieved from

https://www.diffen.com/difference/EQ_vs_IQ

Golis, Chris (2019). A Brief History on Emotional Intelligence. Retrieved by

https://www.emotionalintelligencecourse.com/history-of-eq/

Mayer, Emeran (2011). Gut feelings: the emerging biology of gut-brain communication. Retrieved by

https://www.ncbi.nlm.nih.gov/pmc/articles/PMC3845678/

Mueller, Steve (2018) 40 Character Traits of an Empath. Retrieved by

http://www.planetofsuccess.com/blog/2018/character-traits-of-empaths/

NIH (2019) Mental Illness. Retrieved by

https://www.nimh.nih.gov/health/statistics/mental-illness.shtml

Paul, Margaret (n.d.) What are Emotional Triggers and Why You Need To Understand Them. Retrieved by

https://www.mindbodygreen.com/0-18348/what-are-emotional-triggers-why-you-need-to-understand-them.html

Psychology Today (n.d.) What is Emotional Intelligence. Retrieved from

https://www.psychologytoday.com/us/basics/emotional-intelligence

Pursey, Kirstie (2016) 6 Types of Empaths. Retrieved by

https://www.learning-mind.com/types-of-empaths/

Printed in Great Britain
by Amazon